PUBLIC PHILOSOPHY SOCIETY

Journal of Public Philosophy

Volume 2

Public Philosophy Press

First published by Public Philosophy Press 2021

Phoenix, AZ

Copyright © 2021 by Journal of Public Philosophy

All rights reserved. No part of this publication may be reproduced, stored or transmitted in any form or by any means, electronic, mechanical, photocopying, recording, scanning, or otherwise without written permission from the publisher. It is illegal to copy this book, post it to a website, or distribute it by any other means without permission.

General Editor, Kelly Fitzsimmons Burton

Research Editor, Owen Anderson

Cover art by Beth Ellen Nagle

Typesetting Alyssa Anderson

First edition

ISBN: 978-0-578-76897-7

Contents

Preface   i

Editor's Introduction   iii

Contributors   v

Articles

Pseudo-Intellectuals	O. Anderson	1
Difficult Discussions in Secular Education	K. Burton	15
Contemporary Terrorism's Unholy Trinity	P. Redpath	33
Carl Menger's Objective Value Theory	A. Gastelum	41
The Contemporary Free Will Solution	O. Anderson & M. Nolen	55
Secularization and the Earthly Kingdom	K. Burton	79

Book Reviews

Religion and Science by R. W. Tussing	A. Gastelum	99
Diversity Delusion by H. MacDonald	J. Morgan	103

Preface

The Journal of Public Philosophy is the official publication of the Public Philosophy Society. The goal of the Journal is to publish papers, essays, and book reviews in the mode of classical philosophy. We seek to know the basic truths that are foundational for the common good, and a just and civil society.

The goal of public philosophy is to make the practice of philosophy more accessible and more relevant to students, scholars, and the broadly educated public. We hope to inspire young and old alike in the shared, rational pursuit of wisdom and in love of Being, Unity, the True, the Good, and the Beautiful.

Public philosophy is inspired by Socrates' engagement in dialogue in the agora, the shared public space of the city-state. It is the pursuit of the common good, our shared life together. Currently, we are a group of professors seeking to bring the discussions usually reserved for the classroom into a broader context. We hope that others will join us in an ever-broadening and deepening discussion. The arena for discussions has been college and university public lecture forums, book discussion groups, and campus clubs. We hope that others will expand the public context, perhaps meeting at coffee shops and houses of worship. We have expanded the discussion to an international group with the formation of the Public Philosophy Society.

The Public Philosophy Society is a professional society, offering membership to students, scholars, and educated members of the public. For more information about joining the Society, visit our membership site: https://www.patreon.com/pubphisociety. The Journal of Public Philosophy welcomes submissions for publication by scholars and practitioners in Public Philosophy who share this vision. Submissions may be sent to: info@publicphilosophypress.

com

The Journal of Public Philosophy is published by Public Philosophy Press: www.publicphilosophypress.com

Kelly Fitzsimmons Burton, Ph. D.

General Editor

Editor's Note

Issue 2 of the Journal of Public Philosophy was scheduled to be published in the summer of 2020, but many of our schedules had been disrupted by the Covid 19 global pandemic. Almost all of our contributors are educators, and in March 2020 we were thrown into the world of totally online education. We had to learn new technologies, how to manage working from home, and caring for students and families in new ways. Given this new reality, our priorities shifted, and the Journal was put on hold for a time. As we adjusted to our "new normal" we were able to work together to contribute to our budding new journal.

Hopefully, the Journal is now back on track for regular publication. Please accept our apologies for the late publication of Issue 2, but Issue 3 should be on track for a late summer publication.

In addition to the Journal publication being disrupted by the pan-demic, the Public Philosophy lecture series, out of which the journal articles are solicited, has been totally on hold. We are looking for new ways to do public philosophy. The Public Philosophy Society continues to meet and discuss relevant issues on a monthly basis. We invite you to join our live-online conversations by joining the Public Philosophy Society at: https://www.patreon.com/pubphiso-ciety

Thank you for your support of Public Philosophy.

Yours,

Kelly Fitzsimmons Burton

General Editor

Journal of Public Philosophy

Contributors

Owen Anderson, Ph. D. is Professor of Philosophy and Religious Studies in the New College at Arizona State University. In 2013-2014, he was the William E. Simon research fellow in the James Madison Program at Princeton University and a visiting scholar at Princeton Seminary. He has published seven books including *The Declaration of Independence and God* (Cambridge University Press, 2015) and *The Natural Moral Law* (Cambridge University Press, 2013).

Kelly Fitzsimmons Burton, Ph. D. is a professor of Philosophy and Religious Studies at Paradise Valley Community College in Phoenix, AZ. She is the author of *Retrieving Knowledge: A Socratic Response to Skepticism* (Public Philosophy Press, 2018) and *Reason and Proper Function: A Response to Alvin Plantinga* (Public Philosophy Press, 2019).

Arturo Gastelum is a Ph. D. student in Humanities with an emphasis in Philosophy at Faulkner University. His research interest is in the relationship between faith and reason.

Jason Morgan is Associate Professor at Reitaku University in Chiba, Japan.

Matthew Nolen, Ph.D. has studied the topics of philosophy, theology, and communication for over a decade. He completed his doctoral studies in Communication with a certificate in Asian Studies in 2017. His work has been focused on Strategic Communication. He is a full-time faculty member at Grand Canyon University.

Peter A. Redpath, Ph. D. is retired Full Professor of Philosophy at St. John's University, New York, and is CEO of the Aquinas School of Leadership, Rector of the Adler-Aquinas Institute and Senior Fellow at the Center for the Study of The Great Ideas. He is author of twelve philosophical books [including *The Moral Psychology of St. Thomas Aquinas: An Introduction to Ragamuffin Ethics* (En Route Books & Media, 2017), *A Not-So-Elementary Christian Metaphysics*, Vol. 2

(En Route Books & Media, 2016), and *A Not-So-Elementary Christian Metaphysics*, Vol. 1 (En Route Books & Media, 2nd printing, 2015) and numerous articles and book reviews.

Pseudo-Intellectuals

Owen Anderson, Ph.D.

"You taught me language, and my profit on't is I know how to curse."

"This thing of darkness I acknowledge mine"

In the following I am going to discuss Pseudo-Intellectuals. There is a danger and a delicacy in talking about this topic. The danger is of course that it becomes a type of name calling. Any person someone disagrees with in the academic world can be labeled a pseudo-intellectual. As a kind of ad hominem, it becomes a pseudo-argument like all other forms of that fallacy. It has the appearance of an argument but not the reality. Because of this it is a good example for us as we continue in the study of the "pseudo." There is also the danger of becoming a pseudo-intellectual while trying to identify them. This leads us to the delicacy. In writing about pseudo-intellectuals, the readers can easily wonder if you are speaking about them. This is the wrong approach of course. What we will do in the following is raise our consciousness so that we can better do the work of self-examination. It is taken for granted that no one wants to be a pseudo-intellectual. While we are going to work on identifying what it is to be one, it is up to each of us individually to do the work of self-examination. But enough of dangers and delicacies; we can now get to the subject.

There are already books on the anti-intellectual. But what is the pseudo-intellectual? Pseudo simply means false. So, a false intellectual. But what is an intellectual? How can we tell a real or genuine intellectual from a false intellectual? We will need the real thing to make a comparison. The term denotes one who understands. An intellectual is a person who particularly works in the area of understanding. Now, any field of human work requires understanding. One couldn't build a house or fly an airplane without understanding. But the intellectual is one whose work is in understanding itself. The field is the intellect. For some this might be a temptation toward abstract ideas with little application to the world, and we will look at this as a particular sign of the pseudo-intellectual. The purview of the intellectual is human existence itself. The meaning and purpose of human life. An intellectual might study the non-human, might study physics, chemistry, natural history, but in doing this the intellectual as a human is looking for the meaning to be found in these fields. So, the pursuit of the intellectual is understanding and to understand is to find the meaning in the world.

If the intellectual works to uncover the meaning that is in the world then we know that the pseudo-intellectual is someone who only appears to seek and have meaning. We can't say that the pseudo-intellectual is someone who is merely mistaken about meaning. The pseudo is doing more than making a mistake. The person making a mistake i) can be corrected, and ii) may have various shortcomings or motives that explain the mistake. But in this case the person is still using the intellect in order to make the mistake. By contrast, the pseudo only appears to be using the intellect. And so only appears to have meaning. It is the difference between a mistaken view about what a thing is and the mere appearance, not the reality of a thing.

What is the appearance of meaning without the reality? And who would not know the difference? There is a loss of meaning that comes from the failure to use reason. But there is also a deep need for meaning. One option with the loss of meaning is to recognize one's failure to use reason and repent or change direction. But the other option is to continue without reason, and therefore without meaning, and to attempt to put something else in its place. There is no comparison between meaning and the mere appearance of meaning so that when the former is presented the latter cannot continue.

I've used this term *reason* and said that it is necessary for understanding and meaning. *Reason* is defined as the power of the mind to understand. In itself reason is the laws of thought. These laws are necessary to understand anything because they are that by which we make the distinctions necessary for understanding. These laws are identity (a is a), non-contradiction (not both a and non-a) and excluded middle (either a or non-a). Consider how these are each intertwined (they come as a package that reaffirm each other) and revolve around affirming a thing is what it is and isn't what it isn't.

If we cannot make any distinctions, then we cannot understand. We wouldn't know how what we are claiming to understand is different from anything else. Or if all distinctions are arbitrary or cultural then they are not getting to something real. They might have been other than they are. Or, perhaps including all of these, if there are no clear distinctions then this includes anything we think or say. It is a kind of self-referential absurdity. If we have abandoned reason, then we may not care about contradicting ourselves, but it does mean no one else needs to interact with us. This is the lack of integrity and we need to return to that in a moment.

Let us consider some examples of distinctions we make to illustrate our use of reason. We distinguish God from not God. And we distinguish human from not human. And we distinguish good from not good. We may argue about each of these topics but in any such argument we are presupposing reason and the ability to make distinctions. We may disagree about what it is to be a human, but this disagreement presupposes that there is something called a human that is distinct from non-humans. The life of the intellectual presupposes reason. And this is an indication for us about what the pseudo-intellectual is doing. To attempt the life of the mind apart from the use of reason is a key feature of the pseudo-intellectual.

There are reasons that the pseudo-intellectual might not use reason. One is that the goal has become persuasion. We find this problem very early on in Greek philosophy with the Sophists. That is almost like naming them the Intellectuals, or those who teach wisdom (sophia). But this art was totally reduced to the skill of persuasion. How do you convince an audience to agree with your opinion? Socrates asked if the truth of the opinion mattered and the Sophists didn't seem to think so. You could have a false opinion but the thing to do is to convince others to believe it. The two possibilities there are that you know it is false and that you do not know it is false. One is malicious and the other is culpably ignorant. Much could be said about those but for our purposes we will continue with this problem of persuasion.

The goal of mere persuasion lends itself to the use of informal fallacies. These are pseudo-arguments. Just like the pseudo-intellectual may appear to be an intellectual so too these may appear to be arguments. They can have all the outward trappings of an argument. However, they appeal to something besides reason and a sound argument to support their conclusion. Two of the most commonly used are appeal to pity and appeal to fear. One can appeal to pity to abuse the disposition to compassion in the audience and so work on their empathy to get what you want. Or one can appeal to fear either through a threat (this doesn't work well if you are the one talking to the audience) or through appealing to a threat that everyone is supposed to be afraid of and so getting the audience to do what you want.

The contrast to the use of informal fallacies is the use of reason and argument. There are already good resources about these, and I will not be spending time here teaching of their use (see *Philosophical Foundations* by Surrendra Gangadean). What I do want to highlight here is the role of integrity in distinguishing between the intellectual and the pseudo-intellectual. Integrity is a concern for consistency in what we think, say, and do. The intellectual is one who is saying they are working in the area of the intellect and the goal of that is to understand. Integrity requires being consistent. If what you have is only an opinion, then you do not yet understand. Keep working. But do not present yourself as an intellectual who understands when that is not the case. Or tell your audience this. Say to your audience that you do not understand but you want them to be persuaded of your view in the absence of understanding.

When someone tells us, they understand then we expect them to show that they do indeed understand. This is true in any field. You would expect your accountant to not just claim to know how to do your taxes but to show this as well. Your auto mechanic same thing. So we also expect this of someone who claims to have used their intellect to come to truths about God, human nature, and the good. Show it. And it is in the showing it that they either use reason and argument or they rely on an informal fallacy and reveal themselves to us as pseudo-intellectuals.

What role does reason play in the Academy? The reforms that Socrates introduces which made it possible for his student Plato to found the Academy were certainly in response to the pseudo-intellectuals called Sophists. They taught things like "man is the measure of all things" or "the just person is the one who has power." In one way they were denying reason as ontological (applying to being as well as thought). And they were rejecting reason as transcendental (the highest authority). And they didn't consider reason to be fundamental (not replacing emotions, but fundamental to other aspects of the human personality like emotions and the will). But even if we simply take man as the measure, or power as justice, we can apply reason to these as well to see if meaning has been retained in our opinions. Socrates does this with Thrasymachus in *The Republic* about justice and power.

But the Academy was not built on a solid foundation. Within a few generations it had adopted what has come to be called Academic Skepticism. Because of Platonic assumptions about the forms and knowledge, Academic Skepticism says that knowledge is not possible. We can work back to those assumptions and rethink them to see where the foundation was not in place. But we still have a kind of Academic Skepticism with us today. Knowledge is not possible only probable or plausible. Or knowledge is possible about pragmatic matters because they work but not about things like God, human nature, and the good. How did we end up here again?

One way is by switching from the cognitive to the non-cognitive. This can happen subtly. The intellect has to do with the cognitive and with understanding. When you understand a topic, you can show that you understand. This is usually done through questions and answer (a dialogue, the Socratic dialogues being one example). When someone objects to the connection between understanding and showing they will usually give non-cognitive examples and you see the switch has been made. The non-cognitive involves the emotions/intuitions and the will/practice. These cannot always be put into propositional form. Art and technology are their own unique domains and cannot be reduced to propositions. But because humans need meaning they also cannot avoid the need for interpretation. As soon as we ask "what does this mean" we are now in the cognitive. The intellect operates with beliefs and these have the form of "God is real" or "God is not real." We then support such beliefs with premises that also have that kind of form. But the informal fallacies rely on impressions and feelings. Fear, pity, insults, what is popular, authority. This is the switch to the non-cognitive. The pseudo-intellectual is operating in this non-cognitive realm, denying that we can have knowledge in the cognitive realm, and looking to persuade their audience of their opinion.

It is valuable to note the role of *love* in *philosophy*. The *love* of *wisdom*. Did the Sophists love wisdom? They loved persuasion. But wisdom was not something to be sought if man is the measure of all things. You seek out what you love. I mention this because there are those who might say love is non-cognitive. They may identify it with a feeling or passion. The Greeks famously had different words for different kinds of love. Some Christian authors have picked up on this. What unites them under the term *love* is its focus on what is good. If love is an intense desire for something ("I love it") true love is an intense desire for the good. Or true love of another is an intense desire for the good of that other. So, we see a good example of how the cognitive and non-cognitive work together and how the cognitive gives direction and interpretation to the non-cognitive. Do you love the good? Do you seek the good? I can imagine someone saying, "yes of course." But the follow up question is: "then show me what is good." And here we have the true test. Do you understand the good?

There are two possible directions a person will go in their answer. Yes and no. If they say "yes" then this is simply a matter of having them demonstrate what they claim to understand, and we can see if they have been presumptuous or not. If they say "no" then again there are two ways this works out. One is to take personal responsibility and confess "I should understand the good, but I do not, and it is my fault." With this come consequences especially if the person has put themselves in the place of a public teacher or authority. They will have to confess this to their audience and peers and step back until they understand what they should about the good.

More common is to not take personal responsibility. More common is to blame the good for being too hard to know or even unknowable. Once again this is the Academic Skepticism mentioned above. "I've tried to know the good, but it is unclear." This denial of clarity, at the root of the pseudo-intellectual life, trickles all the way down to the foundation. What is good for a thing is based on the nature of that thing. So, what is good for a human depends on what it is to be a human. Therefore, to say it is not clear what is good is to say it is not clear what is a human. If we know what it is to be a human, then we know what it is good for a human. And it gets worse. Human nature is determined by the Creator of human nature. The claim that it is unclear what is a human is to say that the origin of human nature is unclear. Consider how various theories of origins end up with different views of human nature to make the point (evolutionary, reincarnation, Theistic). To defend the claim that it is unclear what is good the pseudo must then defend the claim that it is unclear what has existed from eternity and is the origin of human nature. Indeed, the pseudo must defend the belief that nothing is clear. We are right back to the idea that all is a matter of opinion and persuasion. Any rally of a defense by saying "but we have statistics, and probabilities, and plausibilities" still falls down on the point that nothing is clear so neither are these.

What does the Pseudo love? Can the Pseudo argue that love is different from non-love? This requires the use of reason. We have the pseudo in focus now. The pseudo has opinions. The pseudo might think these are true or might not think that matters. The pseudo attempts to persuade others to agree with those opinions through the use of pseudo arguments. One more thing to add to distinguish the pseudo from someone who simply has opinion is that they claim to be working in the field of the intellect. Theirs is the world of the intellectual. They derive significance from operating and living in that world. Philosophy, literature, history, the arts. This is why the pseudo initially can fool others because they give the appearance of knowing about the field, we call the humanities. They have many facts ready at hand. One thinks of Gilbert and Sullivan's "Modern Major General" but applied to the humanities. "I am the very model of a modern university professor." Or the Apostle Paul in Athens described in Acts 17. "All the Athenians and the foreigners who lived there spent their time doing nothing but talking about and listening to the latest ideas." The appearance of being an intellectual is attained by being able to talk about the latest intellectual fads and being "in the know."

We spoke above about seeking what we love. This also implies fear. We fear to lose what we love. The love of philosophy comes with the fear of not being wise. And this is because there are consequences either way. There are consequences to being a pseudo intellectual. It might be that the pseudo intellectual denies that there are consequences at least in deed. This is like the Biblical Atheist. This is the one described in Psalm 14; the fool who says there is no god. And the idea isn't simply a materialist who rejects theism. It is the person who denies God as Creator and Redeemer. It is the person who denies that God acts in the world. And this was there from the beginning in the first Biblical Atheist who said to our first parents "you will not surely die." In other words, "wages of sin is not death." Or "there are no consequences, do what you want."

Fear involves recognizing the consequences. This is why the fear of God is the beginning of wisdom. There is awe of God and His works and a sober realization of the consequences in breaking God's law that are summarized under *fear*. We are now linking the pseudo and the fool. I know that both of these are pejorative terms, and I discussed the danger and delicacy of using them at the beginning. They are not to be used lightly or as insults. They are descriptions of real conditions. Unless someone wants to go so far as to deny these ever exist at all then we need to be able to describe them. The arguments may mostly center around who they denote. But that isn't our purpose here and it can mainly be avoided if the primary focus is self-examination and repentance as needed.

The fool is one who thinks he knows and does not know. He makes a statement that is both untrue and significant. "There is no god," or "you will not surely die." These are significant because of their consequences. These are significant because they are demonstrably false. These are significant because we should know they are false. The original temptation was supported by the claim that they could know good and evil as God does. This is an example of denying reason. By reason we know that humans are not God. We know that what has a beginning (a creature) cannot be what is without beginning (the eternal Creator). So, the temptation asked them to deny reason and what is clear about God and man.

This is why I mention it here. This has the appearance of knowledge but not the reality and brings the most dire consequences. Although someone may be deceived by a tempter, they do not lose their own responsibility because this is an example of culpable ignorance. Anyone can think and know that the creature cannot be or become the Creator. What had a beginning cannot be what had no beginning. So, there is the appearance of knowledge ("there is no god") but not the reality. Any basic use of the intellect could have seen this.

The temptation offers a counterfeit. And really the whole subject of a pseudo-intellectual is about counterfeits. In making a counterfeit one wants to make it appear as real as possible without the expense of being real. A counterfeit has failed if it is so accurate it simply is the real thing. That isn't a counterfeit. Instead, something of less value is used to appear to be the same as something of more value. In this case we are talking about a counterfeit intellectual. But because understanding requires showing there is test for counterfeits. This is like the marker used to test dollar bills. It is better than that because it cannot be faked. Well aimed questions expose that this counterfeit cannot explain what they supposedly understand.

Here we might introduce the anti-intellectual. These come in various forms. But there are two I want to bring into this current discussion. These are persons who do not themselves want to do the work of the intellect. These can be called the simple. And one way the simple can respond to the pseudo-intellectual is with awe and respect. This is the exact audience that the pseudo wants and can easily persuade and influence. To this type of simple person, the pseudo appears like the height of human intellectual work. And this popularity and respect go a far way in the mind of other pseudos to give honor that provides the basis for accepting each other.

The other type of anti-intellectual is less impressed with the pseudo. In fact, this one forms a kind of antinomy with the pseudo and they reinforce each other in their disdain. This anti-intellectual can see through the counterfeit nature of the pseudo but makes the mistake of turning away from all of the intellect. The pseudo is successful in persuading this anti that this is the work of the intellect, but this anti has seen through to its valuelessness. The consequence is in reinforcing the anti-intellectual's rejection of the work of the intellect. This rejection of the intellect is seen by the pseudo used to inflate the pseudo's own sense of being intellectual.

Some examples will help us illustrate how the pseudo operates. It won't help for us to name specific beliefs as if they are always held by pseudo-intellectuals. This would give the wrong impression and it would tempt us to stop thinking and instead just look for these beliefs and make the assignation. Rather, the way to proceed here is to show the manner in which a pseudo-intellectual attempts to appear to know while not really knowing. We find this in the use of the informal fallacies as examples of pseudo-arguments. They appear to be arguments in one sense but are not and instead shift to non-cognitive categories like fear or pity. And it is especially this second one that is used by the pseudo-intellectual to advocate for action of some kind.

It often finds its most visible expression in assertions about how to live, what is of value, and causes for activism that are meant to give life significance. And this appearance of significance is what is coupled with the appearance of knowing. The projects of the pseudo-intellectual are put in the language of purpose, dignity, and rights. Perhaps most cherished is love. The goal is to make the world a better place than how you found it. Of course, "better" is precisely what is in contention and in many cases these causes are highly political. But the idea is that the pseudo-intellectual can lecture the rest of humanity on how they ought to live and the causes that count as just.

This is a useful example to begin with because this is the more visible and existential point of contact with the pseudo-intellectual. The pseudo-intellectual relies on the sense of empathy. Empathy involves connecting with the feelings of others. As such it is susceptible to the fallacy of the appeal to pity. Empathy can be misdirected. Empathy is not sufficient to know and do what is just. Empathy is not necessary to know and do what is just. Empathy gives the appearance but not the reality. It is true that there are just causes that should be worked toward. Which ones are they and how should they be worked toward?

What makes this the beginning of examples of the pseudo-intellectual is that it is only the appearance. To have the reality of a just cause one would need to know what is just or what is good. What does it mean to love another? What does it mean to love oneself? Answering these requires showing what is good. Love is seeking the good for another or for oneself. To give the appearance of loving another without showing what is good is not real love.

Answering questions like this is the real use of the intellect. But we will see that when their assertions about what is a just cause are pressed the pseudo quickly turns to skepticism. To know what is just we need to know what is real. Sometimes the pseudo will avoid this by claiming that we don't need to know what is real to help other people. So again, there is an underlying skepticism about knowledge that quickly comes to the surface. The problem is in knowing if we are actually helping or we only think we are helping.

In wanting to know what is real we are asking what is permanent. When something changes, we ask what causes it to change. And when we identify what causes it to change if that also changes, we continue our line of questioning. We are looking for what is unchanging, permanent, real. What is real has existed from eternity without beginning. And this is a good example for us as we identify the pseudo-intellectual. Our use of the intellect should get us to what is real. If it does not, then we are only at the level of appearances. And this is the level of the pseudo-intellectual. Sometimes the pseudo even states that all is change and nothing is permanent. Undaunted by the self-referentially absurd nature of such a belief the pseudo-intellectual makes it foundation on which the rest of the edifice is built. About what is eternal, this pseudo-intellectual says that nothing has existed from eternity. This can be taken in two ways: one, there was once only nothing and then something came into existence or two, there is an eternal line of temporal beings which itself did not have a beginning. The first one is quickly abandoned as it asserts that something came from nothing or that being came from non-being or existence came from non-existence. The second one is simply the belief that all is change and there has always been change. Change is eternal. Only change is real.

Someone could use the intellect to try and defend this position. The pseudo-intellectual comes into our picture when we analyze that defense. To defend this view with the intellect requires the use of reason. By reason we know that *a* is *a*. Being is being and being is not non-being. Being does not come from non-being. This is the use of the intellect to begin to know what is real and what is eternal. The pseudo-intellectual denies that we can use reason to do this. Of course, this is not a merely anti-intellectual denial of reason but is given the appearance of intellectualism. Reason is denied to be ontological; reason does not apply to being as well as thought. And reason is denied to be transcendental; reason is not the highest authority instead some other intuition of the pseudo is a higher authority.

This retreat into skepticism under the denial of reason gets us to the essence of the pseudo-intellectual. The denial of reason is the death of the intellect. If one has integrity one would simply acknowledge this. Some have indeed been consistent in this way and made the move to silence. But the pseudo-intellectual wants to both deny reason and still give the appearance of being an intellectual. This is the counterfeit identified above. Without integrity discussion is impossible.

Integrity can be tested. If we have integrity, we would know what is clear. We would have actually used our intellect to know rather than only appearing to do so. And if we know then we understand. And if we understand then we can reply to questions and show we understand. We expect anyone who claims to understand to be able to show us that they do really understand. And this applies for the intellectual beginning with the first and most basic things.

We are now at the place where we can distinguish between the reality and only the appearance. If someone is using the intellect, then they would know basic things. Even if some were to say they only use the intellect on the very hardest problems, this would mean they are able to very easily use their intellect on these basic matters. To be an intellectual means you use your intellect to know things. To be a pseudo-intellectual means you only give the appearance of using your intellect while not having the reality. And we can take these observations and make this application: if someone is an intellectual, or in the role of a professor or intellectual, then that person should have integrity and be able to show the truth of basic things. These include reason, what is real, and the just life. It is fair to ask people who want us to listen to them these questions; it is our responsibility to do so. In lacking integrity, the pseudo-intellectual will not be able to continue discussion but it is a great benefit for all to have this absence of knowledge exposed.

We can now face what is otherwise delicate to raise. Have you been an anti-intellectual? Have you claimed to know when you don't know? Have you offered yourself as someone who is wise and apologize without the reality of those being present? If so, you can note it, apologize to those you have affected, and begin the work of knowing what is clear about God and the good.

Sometimes this is the explanation of how life makes sense in light of death as the final end of the individual. Or, that this makes sense in light of the absence of God. We can call this first one the "when you're dead you're dead" solution and the second one a kind of atheism that might give a nod to God's existence but denies the power of God to act in this life. The pseudo-intellectual cannot defend these views but says that we do not need to do so we just need to work to help make life better.

Difficult Discussions in Secular Higher Education: Navigating the Streams of Liberal Tolerance and Religious Particularity

Kelly Fitzsimmons Burton, Ph.D.

I: Introduction

There is a preponderance of difficult topics in the headlines today, many of which are related to religion. In addition, there has been a resurgence of religious voices in the public square both nationally and internationally. Often, we don't know how to discuss with one another the underlying assumptions of religiously motivated public actions from partisan voting to suicide bombing. In a world in which one's next-door neighbor may be Buddhist, Hindu, Jewish, Christian, Muslim, New Age, Atheist, or "just shopping around" in the free marketplace of ideas for a religion, it is more important than ever to understand the assumptions of different religions and to have the ability to discuss these assumptions with one another in the public realm in the democratic spirit of the free exchange of ideas and arguments.

Education is one avenue in the promotion of the practice of giving and evaluating reasons. The educational setting is a forum for practicing the skill of public reasoning. The college or university setting is a central location for the discussion of difficult topics, particularly difficult topics dealing with substantive religious claims. I would like to argue that no topic in itself should be ruled out for discussion in the public higher educational setting because it is "difficult." Discussing religious or worldview commitments[1] in the public

---

[1] The definition of "religion" itself is a hotly contested category within the academic study of religion. "Religion," as I am using it, minimally means the belief or

educational setting cannot be avoided in the name of liberal autonomy, neutrality, tolerance, or rationality. The limits of a discussion in the college or university setting are inherent and thus need not be imposed as off limits by educational or legal authorities. To argue this point I will use Jeffery Stout's theory of the secularization of public discourse.

The limits of public discussion are based upon the limitations of a shared discursive practice, rather than based upon some notion of liberal tolerance or secular ideology. I will argue that any topic is legitimate for rational discussion in the classroom. By rational I mean the give and take of reasons for belief and the critical evaluation of those reasons for meaning and coherence and consistency. The limits of discussion are not difficult topics in themselves, but rather the method by which we approach difficult topics. I hope to outline a method by which difficult topics pertaining to religion can be discussed in the higher educational setting.

Educators should not protect students from difficult topics. Rather, students ought to be prepared by educators to engage in the discussion of difficult issues. No topic is too difficult for discussion if there is an agreed upon method by which students and teacher can approach the topic at hand. I propose that a step-by-step approach from more basic assumptions to less basic assumptions can be employed. If the discussion gets hung up on a less basic issue that cannot be resolved, the method is to find a more basic assumption upon which the less basic rests and discuss the more basic first. The discussion can proceed step by step, with the attempt to find agreement or consensus at each step before moving on, from more basic to less basic assumptions. In this way a seemingly difficult topic like the existence of God can be discussed in the public college setting. The most appropriate location within the public college setting for the discussion of difficult religious topics may be in philosophy or

---

set of beliefs by which individuals and groups give meaning to their experiences in the world. The term "worldview" has a similar meaning but is broad enough to include positions without institutional ties such as those that claim to be "spiritual" but not "religious," or those that claim not to believe in God and are thus not "religious" in the traditional sense of having an institutional location. The assumption is that all persons experience the world and must interpret those experiences in light of some belief about the nature of reality. It is in this sense that all persons are "religious" or have a worldview. An inference from this definition of religion is that no one is neutral in respect of worldview or religious assumptions.

religious studies courses. The most appropriate method for discussion may be Socratic dialog where the teacher leads the discussion by asking students to clarify the meaning of the terms that they use.

II: Liberal Tolerance and Education

The notion of allowing substantive religious issues within the secular educational setting may make some persons nervous. One may wonder if the discussion of religion may become the promotion of religion by some educators. Inculcation of students is a vice to be avoided at all costs according to the values of liberalism. In *The Trouble With Principle*, Stanley Fish draws out the implications for the dual goals of maintaining the liberal value of individual autonomy and the necessity of education. He says that:

> If you assume (as most commentators do) that one of the important values supported by the First Amendment is freedom of choice, you will be suspicious of any form of instruction whose intention or effect is to indoctrinate rather to illuminate. That is why the Association of American University Professors, the self-anointed guardian of academic freedom, has always looked askance at religiously based colleges and universities; for rather than being committed to the disinterested play of ideas, they turn out to be very interested in the promulgation of some ideas and the exclusion of some others.[2]

Fish goes on to argue that it is impossible to educate without some form of inculcation – be it religious or otherwise. Furthermore, teaching from the pluralistic liberal model is itself a form of indoctrination. The notion of "openness" and the free play of ideas are values of a liberal worldview.[3] He argues that it is philosophical-

---

2 Fish, Stanley. The Trouble With Principle. (Cambridge: Harvard University Press; 1999), p.153
3 It is not my goal to argue against this liberal model, nor do I deny the benefits

ly impossible to reconcile the First Amendment goals of autonomy with the inevitability of inculcation in education.

A virtue of liberal secular education is that the educator is to remain neutral and as objective as possible in the face of competing views of the good, allowing the autonomous student to freely choose his or her own vision of the good from the free marketplace of ideas. The goal of education, given this model, is to free the student's mind from the chains of tradition and authority. Students should believe based on their critical assessment of a position rather than upon dogmatism or appeals to tradition and authority. It would then make sense for some to be nervous, given this model of education, if teachers are promoting religion in the classroom because teachers would then be appealing to authority rather than to reason. Appeal to dogmatic authority defeats the purpose of a liberal education.

Is it possible to escape from some sort of authority in education? In addition, if students are to autonomously choose some view of the good from the free marketplace of ideas, by what authority will they choose? Choice does not occur in a vacuum. Choice assumes values and values assume some prior conception of the good. Behind this view of the good is a concept of what is real or eternal. This amounts to what some have called a worldview. This is not to say that students are fully conscious of or consistent in the worldview in which they live and breathe, and by which they interpret and make sense of their experiences in the world. Part of this worldview is an epistemological approach to the world, which functions as a source of authority. Students come into the marketplace of ideas with a source of authority and with a conception of the good in place. Students do not come into the classroom as blank slates.

Students are born into a worldview and most likely have learned it through tradition. Students may consciously depart from the worldview in which they were raised. Oftentimes liberal education is seen as the destroyer of the traditions that these students bring to the classroom. How often has it been said by students that they lost their religion when they went to college? How many students can say that they "got religion" while in college? It is often a temptation, if not a stated purpose, of liberal educators to debunk (often in an

---

of such a view. Yet, like all worldviews, it has blind spots and limitations.

authoritarian manner) the authority by which students know and the traditions in which they were raised.

It seems that if liberal educators were to practice what they preach then teachers and students alike would be willing to critically examine together the authorities by which we claim to know. Epistemology is the area of philosophy that has traditionally examined how knowledge is possible. In a philosophy or religion class a discussion could take place in which the topic of religious epistemology is pursued. The question may be asked: Is the authority by which we know personal, textual, intuitional, empirical or rational? Is knowledge of ultimate things even possible at all? These are some difficult topics that need to be explored. These are longstanding difficult topics, which should be an indication that a more basic level of discussion is needed to make progress in these age-old issues.

Is it possible for teachers to come to the classroom as neutral and objective, possessing no worldview of their own by which they interpret and give meaning to the world? Does the teacher lack reliance upon any authority when he/she steps into the classroom? Are the values of a liberal education neutral, or are they part of a worldview that is being presented to the students as neutral? The realization that the answer to these questions is a resounding "no" comes from recent postmodernist criticisms of modern claims to neutrality. Fish states that: "there are no facts without a framework, and any framework you have will have *you*, in the sense of limiting in advance what you can see and think."[4] In an application of this notion to education Stephen H. Webb notes that: "We live in a postmodern world where all levels of education are experiencing a legitimation crisis, so that the source of teachers' authority to make judgments about and evaluations of their students is increasingly unclear."[5] The legitimation crisis in education is due to a lack of a unifying authoritative principle by which teachers can lead students to "truth". Enlightenment appeals to rationality are no longer legitimate appeals to authority in higher education because the way that rationality is defined in the Enlightenment project is itself worldview determined, and as of yet has been unable to withstand the serious objections raised against it.

---

4   Fish, Stanley. Trouble With Principle, p. 159
5   Webb, Stephen H. Taking Religion to School: Christian Theology and Secular Education. (Grand Rapids: Brazos Press; 2000), p. 17

Again, Fish's insightful critique of the liberal ideology of "openness" illuminates how some difficult questions may be allowed and some ruled out of the educational setting on the basis of the educators unnoticed assumptions. He asks:

> What, after all, is the difference between a sectarian school which disallows challenges to the divinity of Christ and a so-called nonideological school which disallows serious discussion of that same question? In both contexts something goes without saying and something else cannot be said (Christ is not God or he is). There is of course a difference, not however between a closed environment and an open one but between environments that are differently closed.[6]

Recognizing the reality of assumptions that both teachers and students bring to the classroom could be one step towards a more realistically "open" discussion. Given the reality that one's worldview will limit the kinds of questions that can be asked because of one's limited range of vision, another step towards engaging difficult discussions in the classroom is to allow for students to raise questions and interact with both fellow classmates and teacher from within their limited range of vision. Recognition of assumptions and the willingness to discuss them openly will allow for a wider range of vision for all involved. If one's goals in teaching are "openness" and that students learn to be "autonomous" thinkers, then this can be a stated goal of the classroom rather than hidden ideology.

The assumptions of teachers can no longer be ignored as influencing the content selection and direction of the courses that they teach. A course is saturated with the worldview assumptions of the teacher. This is unavoidable and it is in this sense that Webb concludes that: "we are all – those of us who teach and study religion – theologians now."[7] He adds that theology is "just another name for the holistic approach to the study of religion, in which students

---
6   Fish, Stanley. Trouble With Principle, p. 156
7   Ibid, p. 17

and teachers come together to probe the mysteries of the divine and seek a public discourse on the many passions that divide us."[8] How we teach and what we teach regarding the existence or non-existence of God makes theologians of us all in that the subject of the divine is unavoidable when teaching religion.

One need not believe in the existence of the divine to "probe the mysteries of the divine." Jürgen Habermas has argued that just as religious believers benefit from secular public reasoning, in a "post-metaphysical world" secularists may also learn from considering religious reasoning. He states in a paper titled "Religion in the Public Sphere":

> ...Post-metaphysical thought is prepared to learn from religion while remaining strictly agnostic. It insists on the difference between certainties of faith and validity claims that can be publicly criticized; but it refrains from the rationalist temptation that it can itself decide which part of the religious doctrines is rational and which part is not. Now, this ambivalent attitude to religion expresses a similar epistemic attitude which secular citizens must adopt, if they are to be able and willing to learn something from religious contributions to public debates - provided it turns out to be something that can also be spelled out in a generally accessible language.[9]

Habermas concludes that it is possible that both those who are committed to secularist and religious positions "face a lack of learning on one or the other side of the religious/secular divide...."[10] In other words, both those committed to either secular or religious worldviews would benefit from learning about and from one another through the free exchange of the give and take of reasoning. If one of the goals of liberal education is "openness," then secular edu-

---
8   Ibid, p. 17
9   Habermas, Jürgen. "Religion in the Public Sphere." Online paper 4/29/06: (www.sandiego.edu/pdf/pdf_library/habermaslecture031105_c939cceb2ab087bdf-c6df291ec0fc3fa.pdf) p. 20.
10   Ibid, p. 21-22

cation should be open to the idea of discussing difficult substantive religious issues in the classroom.

III: Teaching Religion Religiously

If it is impossible for teachers and students alike to be neutral with respect to worldviews/religion, then should the religion teacher "teach religion religiously" as Stephen H. Webb suggests? In *Taking Religion to School* Webb presents a "threefold argument" in which he states that: "the teaching of religion is a religious activity. What a teacher believes about God makes a difference in how she teaches what others believe about God. No teacher of religion can be absolutely neutral toward the topic and be an effective teacher."[11] The second part of his argument states that: "if teaching religion is a kind of religious activity, then it is the utmost importance that teachers think through the intersection of theory and practice, reason and faith in their own lives."[12] The third aspect of Webb's argument is that "if teaching religion is a religious activity, high schools, colleges, and universities need to give more scope for religious voices in the classroom and among religion faculty members."[13]

One may wonder why the teaching of religion must be a religious activity rather than an a-religious one. There seems to be an assumption embedded within Webb's argument that all of life is religious in some sense. Is the critical analysis of arguments for or against the existence of God a specifically religious activity in itself, or for some is it the prolegomena to any religious activity? What if it turns out that through the process of investigation students conclude that there is no evidence for the existence of God? How then would this activity be inherently religious? Is it a religious activity to critically analyze the foundations of religious assumptions for meaning?

Webb argues that teachers of religion should "teach religion religiously, not objectively."[14] This approach may be inferred from the

---

11   Webb, Talking Religion to School, p. 15
12   Ibid, p. 15
13   Ibid, p. 16
14   Ibid, p. 188

notions that all people are religious in that they hold to some worldview, and that no one is "objective" with respect to their interpretation of the world because his/her interpretation will be based upon his/her worldview. Webb is a Christian theologian who seems to struggle with two options with respect to the teaching of religion. One option he envisions is making the classroom a "spiritual place" without making it a "Christian place." The more amorphous "spiritual place" of the classroom is due both to the plurality of his students and the fears of academia of a "Christian imperialism" played out in the classroom. The other option that Webb sees as a possibility for his teaching is the more "objective" approach of teaching "facts" without religious passion.[15] Yet, through a dialog with Webb's fellow educator William C. Placher, a third option for teaching religion is drawn out. Placher states that:

> I suppose my "third way" would consist of coming into the classroom, teachers and students, as the fully human beings we are, including our faith – or lack of it. I agree that the best teaching isn't just reporting facts but creating a space where people can share emotions and beliefs that really matter to us. But I get nervous about the classroom becoming a "spiritual place" ... my real concern is to protect the integrity of faith from being watered down to a generic religiousness."[16]

Placher's approach seems to be more consistent with the liberal ideal of the free exchange of ideas and the give and take of reasoning. He also seems more conscious of protecting the separation of church and state in his desire to "protect the integrity of faith." In his theory of teaching religion religiously, Webb seems to advocate more than the free exchange of ideas. He seems to advocate a particular tradition from which to teach religion religiously. One may wonder if he would equally advocate a Muslim theologian, teaching religion religiously in the secular academy. Would he allow for a Hindu professor to teach religion religiously?

---

15   Ibid, p. 192
16   Webb, Taking Religion to School, p. 191

It may be that the context in which Webb teaches allows for a community of shared values which is more conducive to "creating a spiritual place" in the classroom than other secular educational settings. Rather than saying that Webb's position is wrong and ought not to be advocated, in the spirit of diversity his position should be allowed as one among many possible ways of teaching religion. Advocating "teaching religion religiously" may be more a matter of wisdom, context, and the needs of students rather than a matter of "wrong" pedagogy. In the secular educational setting Webb's position should be given just as much freedom of expression as that of alternative secular approaches to religion.

While agreeing in principle about much of what Webb says regarding the necessity of the teaching of religion, I have doubts about the wisdom of Webb's practice of teaching religion religiously. The reason for this is that I think that teaching religion religiously begins with assumptions about the divine and about how the divine is to be approached, rather than exploring the question as to whether we can know the divine at all or whether something divine exists and what he/she may be like. Webb's position, at least as he has expressed it in *Taking Religion to School,* does not seem to get back to what is more basic in a discussion. He argues well that no one is neutral with respect to religion. All have a "faith" by which they view the world. Yet is it possible to step back and critically analyze one's faith? Is it the job of the philosophy or religion teacher to assume a particular position, or should he/she subject his/her own position to rational scrutiny in the process of teaching?

Webb seems to want to meet students where they are in their thinking, but does he want to take them back to more basic questions? Is he willing to entertain the idea that he may have to adjust his position when faced with objections by his students? Is his position too partisan from the start? By partisan I mean assumed without proof or the possibility of proof. Partisanship in pedagogy does seem to be an implication of some postmodern theories – people find themselves with a worldview, but that worldview cannot itself be proven. Webb draws from some aspects of postmodern theory throughout the book. Is this an assumption that he would accept? Does Webb's position, stemming from Christian Theology, rely upon scripture as an authority and would he bring scriptural claims into the classroom?

It is possible for reason and faith to be brought into the classroom without appeal to scriptural claims. Historically, Natural Theology has been a tool to deal with these questions. Arguments drawing on general revelation can be used without appeal to scriptural authority.[17] Webb does not mention this distinction, but I wonder if it would benefit his position to consider its pedagogical usefulness. General revelation is more basic and logically prior to scripture, or what has been called special revelation. General revelation, since it is less particularistic, can be a valuable tool for any religion to bring to bear both in the classroom and in public discourse subjected to "public reason giving." Reasoning in terms of general revelation seems to be a lost skill of the theologian, the revival of which would go a long way in creating a space for religious voices to address a pluralistic public.

IV: An Alternative

Has public discourse been secularized? Must the discourse of the public classroom be secular – that is – neutral with respect to comprehensive religious claims? Jeffrey Stout's "account of secularization":

> Concerns what can be taken for granted when exchanging reasons in public settings. A setting is public in the relevant sense if it involves no expectation of confidentiality and if it is one in which citizens address one another qua citizens. What makes a form of discourse secularized, according to [his] account, is not the tendency of the people participating in it to relinquish their religious beliefs or to refrain from employing them as reasons. The mark of secularization, as [he] use[s] the term, is rather the fact that participants in a given discursive practice are not in a position to take for granted that their interlocutors

---
[17] A theology of general revelation includes what all persons can know about God by reasoning about the creation, whereas special revelation is redemptive in character and is what can be known by God's special communication with human beings.

are making the same religious assumptions they are. This is the sense in which public discourse in modern democracies tends to be secularized.[18]

Secularization of public discourse then "is simply a matter of what can be presupposed in a discussion with other people who happen to have different theological commitments and interpretive dispositions."[19] Stout argues further that:

> Public ethical discourse in modern democratic societies tends not to presuppose agreement on the nature, existence, and will of God. Nor does it presuppose agreement on how the Bible or other sources of religious insight should be interpreted. As a result, theological claims do not have the status of being "justified by default" – of being something all participants in the discursive practice are effectively obligated to defer to as authoritative or justified. And this consequence of theological plurality has an enormous impact on what our ethical discourse is like. It means, for example, that in most contexts it will simply be imprudent, rhetorically speaking, to introduce theological premises into an argument intended to persuade a religiously diverse public audience.[20] (Stout, p. 98-99)

Stout's analysis of the secularization of public discourse seems to make sense logically and it can be empirically verified. Yet, one may affirm on the one hand the rhetorical lack of wisdom to "presuppose agreement on the nature, existence, and will of God" in public discourse, while on the other asking where do citizens hash out differences in understanding the "nature, existence, and will of God?" Do we just take it for granted that these are intractable differ-

---

18   Stout, Jeffrey. Democracy and Tradition. (New Jersey: Princeton University Press; 2004), p. 97.
19   Ibid, p. 97
20   Stout, Democracy and Tradition, p. 98-99

ences and are forever off limits because agreement is impossible? Do we retreat into our respective fideistic and skeptical corners? It is possible to discuss these difficult topics in the classroom setting even while recognizing the reality of the secularization of public discourse.

Allowing for the discussion of substantive religious issues within the classroom can serve the dual purposes of preparing students for appropriate public debate and allow for students to explore and develop reasons for their own religious beliefs, or lack thereof. Within the classroom students can "try out" the practice of public discourse about religious assumptions and see why some arguments do or do not work. In this setting students, directed by their instructor, can help one another hone their skills of identifying and articulating religious assumptions and critically examining those assumptions for meaningfulness. The first application of this method, both for the teacher and students, should be self-examination of one's own position. The teaching of religion should help students to become more conscious of and more consistent in their own worldview, in addition to helping them to understand that of their neighbor.

In this way students don't have to "check their faith at the door" of the classroom, but rather they should be encouraged to bring their faith in all of its particularity and be willing to critically examine it for meaning. The Presuppositional approach that I endorse would say that meaning is more basic than truth and so the meaning of religious or worldview assumptions should be tested prior to the truth-value of those assumptions. For instance, students can be asked to articulate what they mean when they say, "God exists." What do they mean by "God?" Will the Jewish, Christian, Muslim, Mormon, or Hindu student have the same understanding of the nature of "God?" The teacher could explore the relationship between faith and reason by asking students what their understanding of "faith" is and what their understanding of "reason" is. Different understandings could be identified and the class as a whole, though a process of critical examination of the concepts, could have a conversation as to why certain formulations of "God" or "faith" or "reason" are more coherent than others.

The goal of this kind of discussion is to get students to first identify and articulate their own assumptions and then to critically analyze them for meaning and rational coherence. Students will then be in a better place to see why some of their assumptions may or may not be useful in a broader public discourse. Students may find out that sometimes it is helpful to keep certain aspects of religion private; while at other times they may find that a public religious voice is necessary.

This approach to religious assumptions in the classroom is risky in two ways: on one hand it may cause students to have doubts about what they thought they previously understood regarding their religion/worldview. On the other hand, it may bring about stronger religious conviction as they find tools for supporting the belief that they hold. Yet, this is the risk of a liberal education and students learning to subject religious assumptions to critical scrutiny.

Secular ideology is not the logical outcome of a liberal education. For instance, in a philosophy of religion course, given an honest and critical engagement, it is possible that a student may come away with what he/she believes provides proof for the existence of God. It is also possible that an honest engagement with the problem of evil can shake a student's beliefs to the core. What happens when students who assume the very existence of the external world encounter the notion that the world might possibly be an illusion, as in Advaita Vedanta or Idealist Philosophy? Should secular liberal education protect students from these possible life- altering encounters with difficult substantive religious issues?

V. Conclusion

The limits of discussion of difficult topics in the secular public higher educational setting stem from the limits of our worldview assumptions and methodological approaches, rather than from the difficulty of the topics themselves. A full and open engagement with difficult religious issues may be limited by educators who are committed to a strict adherence to the liberal claims of neutrality, autonomy, tolerance and rationality. As Stanley Fish has noted, difficult religious discussions are often disallowed in secular education in the name of tolerance. The assumption is that religion is inherently divisive and in the name of tolerance for one another religion ought to be kept private while more "rational" topics may be discussed in the classroom. Yet, what one considers "rational" is often relative to one's religious/worldview assumptions. Therefore, disallowing the discussion of difficult substantive religious topics in the secular classroom on the basis of liberal tolerance or "rationality" are not legitimate pleas.

On the other hand, approaching the teaching of religion religiously may introduce a religious particularity into the classroom that assumes less basic religious claims with which most students will not be able to relate. Although this approach may not be "wrong," it may be pedagogically unwise and unfruitful in some contexts. Teaching religion religiously may be unwise for the same reason that speaking with religious particularity in the public realm may be rhetorically ineffective due to the secularization of public discourse. The shared discursive practices of a given class will depend upon the shared assumptions of the students and teacher within that class. Given the possibility of maximally shared assumptions, minimally shared assumptions, or something in between, a teacher should be able and willing to meet the students where they are and help to foster a shared discussion in which all who are willing may participate.[21]

A Presuppositional approach to the teaching of religion will meet students where they are and, depending on the context, either pull the discussion back to more basic assumptions, or move forward from more basic issues upon which sufficient agreement has been established to a discussion of less basic issues. A Presuppositional approach to the discussion of difficult religious topics can chart a course between the rough waters of secular liberal ideology and religious particularity. This approach does not require the relinquishing of a liberal approach to education. It does require a rethinking of the secular liberal approach insofar as it claims to be neutral, "rational," free of authority, or exclusionary of views that challenge liberal ideology. A Presuppositional approach to discussion may uphold the liberal virtues of critical inquiry, public reason

---

[21] I should stipulate at this point that not all students will want to discuss religious/worldview assumptions, just as not all individuals want to discuss religion in the public realm. It may be that some students are more comfortable keeping their views private.

giving, and autonomous[22] thinking. Yet it also allows for students to retain their particular worldview or religion, even brining those very assumptions to the table as subject matter for class discussion. A Presuppositional approach to discussing substantive religious topics may require a teacher with deeply held religious assumptions to use the theological tool of general revelation or to translate particular assumptions into a more commonly shared discourse so as to create a shared discursive practice within the classroom.

Finally, it must be acknowledged that it is impossible for both students and teachers to "leave their faith at the door" when they enter into the classroom. Religious/worldview assumptions can be a hindrance to discussion, but they are not necessarily so. Any and every difficult topic ought to be allowed within the secular public educational setting. Progress in discussion will be made provided there is an agreed upon method for discussion. I propose that a Presuppositional method is a desired approach for the discussion of difficult religious topics. Students can practice a Presuppositional approach to discussion and the public giving of reasons for religious beliefs in the context of the classroom, and hopefully carry that approach with them when they participate in discussion in the broader public sphere.

---

[22] Thinking is autonomous in a limited sense. One must acknowledge that one cannot escape from some form of authority stemming from worldview assumptions. Yet, one can learn to think critically about one's assumptions, even thinking critically about one's source of authority itself.

Bibliography

Fish, Stanley. *The Trouble With Principle*. (Cambridge: Harvard University Press; 1999)

Habermas, Jürgen. "Religion in the Public Sphere." Online paper 4/29/06:

(www.sandiego.edu/pdf/pdf_library/habermaslecture031105_c939cceb2ab087bdfc6df291ec0fc3fa.pdf)

Stout, Jeffrey. *Democracy and Tradition*. (Princeton: Princeton University Press; 2004)

Webb, Stephen H. *Taking Religion to School: Christian Theology and Secular Education*. (Grand Rapids: Brazos Press; 2000)

Contemporary Terrorism's Unholy Trinity: Utopian Dreams, Victimhood, and Systematic Evil

Peter A. Redpath, Ph. D.

I would like to start my talk today by referring to Italian Existentialist Nicola Abbagnano's 1980 book *The Human Project: The Year 2000* (*L'uomo progetto 2000*). I do so because, in this work, I think Abbagnano displays some perceptive insights about the nature of contemporary terrorism and how it radically differs from its nineteenth-century counterpart.[1] Abbagnano sees nineteenth-century terrorists aspiring to be heroes, attempting to "vindicate the oppressed, and, at any moment, ready to sacrifice themselves for this task." They "picked as their victims only the most noteworthy power symbols: sovereigns, princes, prime ministers, and so on." In contrast to these terrorists, Abbagnano contends that, ultimately, for contemporary terrorists, *individual* "oppressed and oppressors do not exist.... Only the System that must be discarded exists, to be put out of commission to hasten its demise."[2]

Abbagnano maintains that contemporary "[t]errorists are not assassins murdering for sadistic pleasure, or beasts that have given in to their bloody instincts. They are lucid people pursuing an objective that, for them, is intrinsically good: destruction of a bad society to construct upon its ruins a society devoid of its defects." These terrorists possess a perfect logic, of false absolutes: "Absolutism of the lack of hope lies at the root of terrorism: negation of hope in the ability, somehow from within and by means of tools that society makes available to its members, to modify society by com-

---
1 Nicola Abbagnano, *The Human Project: The Year 2000*, ed. Nino Langiulli, trans. Nino Langiulli and Bruno Martini (Amsterdam and New York: Editions Rodopi, B.V., in press); *L'uomo progetto 2000* (Rome: Dino Editori, 1980).
2 Ibid., p. 45.

bating the evil that nestles within its structure." Those attracted to contemporary terrorism "think that any correction of the System is impossible. The System would eventually trivialize the correction through its infernal mechanism. The mechanism always acts as a robot whose primary objective is its own conservation."

Hence, contemporary terrorists come "to identify this society purely and simply with Evil. When we opt for a direct confrontation with Evil, we do not come to terms. We try, instead, to destroy it with every possible means."[3] Like the very System they oppose, Abbagnano claims that today's terrorists are utopian dreamers:

> The terrorist utopia is the current form of the always-recurring myth in human history: a fabulous Eden. In absolutizing this utopia, terrorists can feel that they act in good faith, as does a surgeon forced to operate on a sick body to save it from certain death. They cannot, must not, have pity. Their duty is one alone: to sink the scalpel into the wound, cut away the diseased flesh, and excise the organ where it nestles.[4]

Abbagnano thinks that an existential revolt, a false absolutization of a perfect model of human existence, is intrinsic to the terrorist utopian dream. He believes that false absolutization leads today's utopian terrorists "to fall into the exact same sin that they ascribe to the society against which they take up arms, an absolutized permissiveness that leads to tolerance of nothing, to the inflexibility of the closed project, that does not foresee or accept modifications."[5]

He maintains that terrorists think that something is wrong with contemporary society conceived after the fashion of a System. Somewhat like a political puritan, the contemporary terrorist sees the System as a permissive society that, by tolerating everything, is pure evil. Like many people caught within such a society, terrorists will "accuse such a society of being in reality tyrannical, oppressive, totalitarian in its alienating structure. That transforms human be-

---

3   Ibid., p. 44.
4   Ibid., p. 45.
5   Ibid.

ings into objects, merchandise, anonymous cogs in an anonymous machine." As Abbagnano says: "The point remains: permitting everything is tantamount to permitting nothing."

In such a society, Abbagnano thinks we all become consumers, victims, inert links in a chain moved by the goals of the System. The System extrinsically determines all the links of the chain to cooperate. Each of us has value to the extent that we serve the unstoppable and predestined progress of the System. As individuals we are insignificant, have no worth. We must tolerate every external pressure because the Scientific Social System grows through our increasing consumption of tolerance, absolute permissiveness, increasing elimination of anything different from the System. Thus, we obtain significance by absorbing into ourselves, consuming, the unity we obtain from being part of the System's progress.[6]

Abbagnano contends that the utopian dream of contemporary terrorists is a kind of millennialism, a utopianism. However, he does not limit such millennialism to religion. He says a "secular millennialism" also exists "that precludes any transcendent perspective." As an example, he gives the "Marxist dream of realizing an Earthly Paradise:"

Abbagnano claims the Italian Communist Party was the incarnation of Stalin's myth.[7] Once Stalin's myth died, so did the Party. In Italy, this caused a simultaneous politicization of Catholic masses proposing their own version of millennialism (by which I presume Abbagnano means "liberation theology" or versions of socialist theologies of Catholic action) in which they expected "a reign of justice soon to be established on Earth under the sign of a new Christ, immanentistically dropped into history." He maintains that Italian Catholics considered this movement as "a concrete alternative to Marxist Messianism, if not actually a collaboration with it for the sake of a goal regarded as common: rescue of human beings from industrial alienation."

According to Abbagnano, a convergence of these two dispersals caused the phenomenon of terrorism to mature in Italy. More precisely, it started from that part of the phenomenon that arises and develops as global contestation of the System in the name of a new

---

6   Ibid., p. 44.
7   Ibid., pp. 46-47.

society to be built on its ruins, starting obviously from scratch and with a totally different objective. We arrive at the scorched earth of the Red Brigades, and of all those other terrorist organizations that proclaimed to fight for a better society: at the terrorism of millennialist inspiration. A millennialism exquisitely political....[8]

In my opinion, Abbagnano presents an understanding of contemporary Western terrorism that is largely correct, gives us helpful information for comprehending the current clash of forces that is dramatically changing the world around us: a global contest of millennial terrorist inspiration against the Western political System and the Western political System against the System of Islamo-fascism. While we can reasonably say that the terrorists engaged is the suicide bombings of the World Trade Center in 2001 were religious fanatics, utopian dreamers, I concur with Abbagnano that blind religious fanaticism does not explain the hatred of the West of millennial terrorist leaders like bin Laden. More than Christianity or Judaism, these leaders hate the evil social System that they think contemporary Christianity and Judaism represent and promote: a secular, permissive millennial fundamentalism that they, mistakenly, but with some justification, identify with the entire Western political order and pure evil.

Mostly anyone familiar with modern Western culture knows that the modern tendency to view reality in terms of a System started with René Descartes's *dream* to transcend the Renaissance animism, skepticism, and superstition that had retarded development of mathematical physics in the West. To transcend this situation, Descartes co-opted and secularized St. Augustine's famous method of faith seeking understanding and transposed it into a universal methodic doubt whereby he supposedly was able to free himself from centuries of bad learning habits and scientific superstition. By eliminating these bad habits that distracted his will and caused it to wander, Descartes claimed to have discovered an innate system of clear and distinct ideas that God had buried in his mind. This "system" of clear and distinct ideas, or body of knowledge, constituted true knowledge and true science, which, for the first time since the start of the human race, Descartes supposedly had discovered.

In short, Descartes had claimed that he had discovered *the meth-*

---

[8] Ibid., p. 47.

od of achieving all knowledge and science, and that this science consisted in a body of knowledge that had lain hidden within his soul for years and within Western culture for centuries. Thus, true science was a set of revealed truths that, because of his exceptional ability to focus the attention of his will on his own ideas, especially upon his metaphysical ideas of God, self, and the world, Descartes was able to reach through a kind of secular faith seeking understanding.

The partial success and failure of the Cartesian project is no secret to anyone familiar with the history of modern philosophy. Descartes's method was supposed to provide the philosophical foundation for modern physics, was supposed to reduce the whole of science to mathematical physics and its systematic grounding in the Cartesian method.

Descartes, however, failed to achieve these goals. This failure left the claims of modern science with no philosophical grounding. At best, the exaggerated claims of the Cartesian project and of modern physics to constitute the whole of human knowledge, art, and science were gratuitous, grounded on nothing more than dreams, fideism, sophistry, poetry, and deconstructed, secularized theology, propaganda.[9]

Since Descartes had failed to give a rational justification for his exaggerated claims about mathematical physics and science, several thinkers sympathetic to his project attempted to do this for him. Chief among them was Jean-Jacques Rousseau.[10]

By the time Rousseau came on the scene, he realized that the attempt to salvage Descartes' view of science as a totally given body, or system, of clear and distinct ideas had to be scrapped. Using Descartes's method, no way existed to reconcile the contradictions inherent in Descartes's justification of physical science in terms of a self-revealed system of already-given clear and distinct ideas. Hence, Rousseau partly abandoned and reconstituted the Cartesian project.

---

9   For a detailed critique of Descartes and his method, see my *Cartesian Nightmare: An Introduction to Transcendental Sophistry* (Amsterdam and Atlanta: Editions Rodopi, B.V., 1997).
10   For a detailed critique of these attempts to repair the Cartesian "system," see my *Masquerade of the Dream Walkers: Prophetic Theology from the Cartesians to Hegel* (Amsterdam and Atlanta: Editions Rodopi, B.V. 1998.

To salvage the notion of science as a system, Rousseau transformed Descartes's dream into a utopian project, a utopian dream. He rejected Descartes's claims that science was an already given, system of clear and distinct ideas buried in the human mind, until someday clarified by a heroic figure like Descartes employing universal methodic doubt. In place of these claims, Rousseau "resigned himself to accept that" at least in their inception, "modern philosophy's principles are essentially dualistic, animistic, and obscure."[11] He then designed his own sort of secularized theology, or utopian mythology, to explain how systematic, absolutized science emerges totally out of human beings from systems of obscure feelings.[12]

In my opinion, this secularized theology, utopian mythology, constitutes the Enlightenment spirit and the secular millennialism that Abbagnano has identified as the false absolutism of the closed project that is the source of contemporary Western terrorism: a utopian dream mistakenly confounded with a metaphysical idea and transformed into the highest goal of practical reason and moral and political life, "the myth of an inevitable and unstoppable progress" of absolutized science.

In my opinion, also, this secular millennialism, this utopian myth, is in no way essential to Western culture. It is essential to Western socialism, contemporary Progressive Liberalism.

Rousseau started this utopian myth by maintaining that "only spirits are substances," only spirits exist, and "even apparently inanimate beings, like stones, are animate. They are sensitive, but have no sensation, much as we might consider an angel to be animate if we were to think of it as a pure intellect empty of ideas."[13]

Given this pan-spiritualism, in his classic work *Emile or On Education*, Rousseau incorporated the now-famous Western ideas of "progress" or "development" and "tolerance" into a secularized theological understanding of learning that viewed all intellectual development to result from a psychological conflict in which human beings work together with an internal teacher, the voice of God, or

---

11 Redpath, *Masquerade of the Dream Walkers*, p. 91. See, also, Jean-Jacques, *Emile or On Education*, trans. Allan Bloom (New York: Basic Books, Inc., Publishers, 1979), p. 274.
12 Redpath, *Masquerade of the Dream Walkers*, pp. 66-99.
13 Rousseau, *Emile*, pp. 270-274.

conscience. Rousseau uses this internal conflict to explain how science as a system of clear and distinct ideas comes into being from previously multiple and obscure ideas.

In this work *Emile*, Rousseau's procedure is to have Emile, or Abstract Man, totally emerge out of himself into the system of Enlightened science. Emile does this through a three-stage projection of his emotions, or passionate imagination, under the necessary voice of conscience to progress or develop from a totally selfish and emotional animal being through the ever-widening principle of tolerance into a totally moral, civil, enlightened, and selfless being.

Clearly, Rousseau's "philosophy" is little more than a millennial animism, a utopian, myth about human origins, grafted onto Descartes's dream of science as an enlightened system of ideas. This pseudo-philosophy, secularized religion, is the essence of modern Western socialism. In Rousseau's utopia, moral and political notions like the voice of conscience, development, progress, and tolerance become transmogrified into neo-Averroistic metaphysical principles of modern socialism to justify a fideistic view that systematic science is a divine, millennial project that constitutes human destiny. Metaphysics and philosophy, thereby, become utopian political projects of an enthused poetic imagination emerging to systematic scientific self-awareness through progressive projection and conflict with its own emotional self-revelation and development, the same enthused spirit that, *mutatis mutandis*, reappears in Marx's utopian dream of a classless society, the conflict between the proletariat and bourgeois, and, as Abbagnano says "the salvific coming of Comrade Stalin."

This utopian dream generated Fascism, Nazism, and Marxism as necessary means to continue acceptance of its myth of unstoppable progress of absolutized science. This utopian dream of an inevitable and unstoppable progress of absolutized systematic science is a first principle of modern Western terrorism, which most of us today call "socialism." This disordered, fundamentalistic, crusading spirit of the Enlightenment project is, knowingly or not, the ultimate ground of the System that is the primary object of hatred by millennial Islamic terrorists. Not to understand that this myth is the chief object of Islamic hatred will cause Westerners and non-Westerners to misunderstand our terrorist enemies, and, worse still, to misunderstand ourselves and the main cause of the global changes that are presently taking place around us.

Peter A. Redpath

Plenary Session Address

Man in Culture Annual World Congress

John Paul II Catholic University of Lublin

15 April 2009

Carl Menger's Objective Value Theory: Menger's Undeveloped Contribution to Economics

Arturo Gastelum

Introduction

Carl Menger (1840-1921) stands as a seminal figure in the history of economic thought. He is credited with the development of subjective value theory in what became known as "The Marginalist Revolution" through the publication of Principles of Economics in 1871. Subjective value theory moved economics from accounting for value by quantitative factors—gold for Mercantilism, land for Physiocracy, labor for Karl Marx, and cost of production for Adam Smith and Classical Economists—to subjective value where ultimately the individual's beliefs regarding the good provide the value of economic goods and services. According to Menger, "The determining factor in the value of a good, then, is neither the quantity of labor or other goods necessary for its production nor the quantity necessary for its production, but rather the magnitude of importance of those satisfactions with respect to which we are conscious of being dependent on command of the good."[1] This represented a revolution in economic understanding of valuation. Since Menger's formulation of subjective value theory, modern economics has presuposed it as the proper paradigm to understand value which as a result stopped any further inquiry into objective value theory. The latter is Menger's other contribution—arguably of far greater significance—of formulating the basis for an objective value the-

---

1   Carl Menger, *Principles of Economics* (Auburn: Ludwig von Mises Institute, 2007), 147.

ory. Unfortunately, Menger's contribution remained undeveloped by Menger himself, Eugen von Bohm-Bawer, his closest disciple in Basic Principles of Economic Value (1886) and by Ludwig von Mises, the greatest systematizer of Austrian Economics in his magnum opus—Human Action: A Treatise on Economics (1949). Since the Marginalist Revolution, economics became fixated on a phenomenological understanding of value at the expense of an objective value theory where the origin and nature of value were to be accounted in ontology, metaphysics and normative ethics. By closely analyzing the insights provided in Principles of Economics, it will be shown that Menger laid the basis for an objective value theory rooted in metaphysical claims that have normative ethical implications for understanding the nature of wealth and human progress. In addition, it will be explained how Mises set aside Menger's objective value theory due to skepticism rooted in faulty epistemic assumptions. The effect of the rejection of objective value theory has had a detrimental effect on the development of economics as a science; its ability to provide a meaningful account of human action in light of the good; and its witness in addressing public disputes between socialism and capitalism that have plagued modern society. Ultimately, it will be shown that uncritically held assumptions on more basic beliefs regarding epistemology (the possibility of knowledge), metaphysics (the nature of reality), and ethics (rational justification for the good) limited economists to remain within the confines of phenomenology and descriptive explanations.

Menger's Objective Value Theory in *Principles of Economics*

Carl Menger sought to uncover the underlying laws of economics which are true and universally applicable. He attempted to prove axiomatically from self-evident principles that there exist certain fixed features of reality which are and will always be true of human nature. This was his objective in writing *Principles of Economics:* "It is the task of the reader to judge..., whether I have been able to demonstrate successfully that the phenomena of economic life, like those of nature, are ordered strictly in accordance with definitive laws."[2] This concern with universally true conclusions corresponding with the nature of reality sets aside Mengerian economics from other modern economists.

Menger begins his inquiry into the nature of economic principles by adopting the principle of causality as the cornerstone. In seeking to erect a systematic account of economic knowledge, Menger sees the need to find an indubitable foundation able to account for subsequent knowledge. According to Menger, causality is self-evident; it is a necessary precondition for intelligibility. Its denial would render economic phenomenon and human action meaningless. He describes the principle as follows: "All things are subject to the laws of cause and effect. This great principle knows no exemption, and we would search in vain in the realm of experience for an example to the contrary."[3] It is important to note that Menger places the principle of causality beyond empirical deniability; it is not a truth arrived by experience but precedes it, hence rendering it an *a priori* truth of reason. Through the adoption of this principle as an indubitable truth of reason, Menger will proceed to link the law of cause and effect with knowledge and human progress. Cause and effect link human wants in the individual as well as the great universal structure of relationships among human beings.[4] Passing from the state of want to its satisfaction requires a sufficient cause for this change to occur. Therefore, understanding of human fulfillment in the attainment of happiness will likewise necessitate factoring the principle of causality as an explanatory tool.[5] Menger employs the principle of causality to provide an essential definition of how a potential good acquires its good-character. How a good goes from potentiality to actuality. This fourfold description seeks to grasp the essence of the good-character of all goods which will serve as the source to understanding wealth and its accumulation in human progress. The four components include a human need, causal connection between the object and the fulfillment of the human need, knowledge of this causal connection, and command to satisfy that need.[6] All of these four components must be present for a good to

---

2   Guido Hulsmann, *Mises: The Last Knight of Liberalism* (Auburn: Ludwig von Mises Institute, 2007), 48.
3   Menger, *Principles of Economics*, 51.
4   Ibid.
5   Ibid., 52.
6   Menger, *Principles of Economics*, 52.

acquire its good-character and be able to serve in the satisfaction of our needs— "Only when all four of these prerequisites are present simultaneously can a thing become a good. When even one of them is absent, a thing cannot acquire good-character."[7] By implication, if we as humans are to attain what we perceive to be good, or what will make us happy, these four good-character criteria will have to be observed. It is a law in accordance with Menger, its violation would lead to unrealizing the attainment of what we desire, in which case the uneasiness (dissatisfaction) will remain until those four requirements are fulfilled.

It is at this point that subjective value theory and the objective value theory converge. Subjective value theory requires that the individual becomes aware of a need; that the potential good has the inherent properties to be brought into causal connection with the satisfaction of a need; that the individual becomes aware of the causal connection between the need, the good, and its ability to satisfy that need; and that the individual has command over the good to satisfy the human need. The qualities to become a good-character are inherent in the object, but the subjective satisfaction of the individual can only occur once the thing acquires the good-character. Here lies a critical distinction between the objective and subjective components of Menger's contribution. Something may objectively have capabilities to fulfill our needs, yet our subjective ignorance of the causal connection between the object and our desire will lead us to not see its true value. This gives rise to the distinction between 'real' and 'imaginary' goods. Menger explains that an imaginary good has two components which by implication violate the nature of reality: "When attributes, and therefore capacities, are erroneously ascribed to things that do not really possess them, or when non-existent human needs are mistakenly assumed to exist."[8] According to Menger, human beings have both real and imaginary needs. A real or actual need is one that arises from human nature and corresponds to the nature of the world while an imaginary or mistaken need does not correspond with the nature of reality. Real needs correspond to an objective value theory where goods are appraised in accord with their reflection of reality while imaginary goods are mistaken for, they are rooted in a false understanding of the world which acts contrary to the objective improvement of human nature. Humanity

[7] Ibid.
[8] Menger, Principles of Economics, 53.

has a long and ample history of engaging in the pursuit of imaginary goods—belief in false metaphysics (polytheism, animism, pantheism, etc.) and by seeking to find lasting happiness in objects of desire that are not connected with the ultimate.

Knowing the distinction between real and imaginary goods will depend upon our understanding of the true composition of things, in other words in truly grasping the essential qualities of a being which presupposes an accurate understanding of the world, i.e., a worldview or metanarrative that best resembles reality. This is Menger's metaphysical insight that brings forth the objective value theory capable of accounting for true wealth and societal progress. Knowledge of reality is the highest source of wealth since it unlocks the latent good-character in the nature of things; the greater the understanding of the nature of things, the greater the number of goods available to enhance human flourishing individually and collectively. Menger infers a correlation between knowledge and progress and lack of knowledge and a corresponding lack of progress: "As people attain higher levels of civilization, as men penetrate more deeply into the true constitution of things and of their nature, the number of true goods becomes constantly larger, and as can be understood, the number of imaginary goods becomes progressively smaller."[9] In other words, there is a causal connection between knowledge and wealth; the greater the knowledge the greater the wealth attainable. Here wealth is designated to refer to all the true goods necessary to satisfy the longing of human nature for fulfillment in all areas of life; both tangibles and intangibles. Likewise poverty in a culture is a reflection of the culture's lack of understanding of reality: "The quality of consumption goods at human disposal are limited only by the extent of human knowledge of the causal connection between things, and by the extent of human control over these things."[10] What accounts for the present state of affluence in the modern world which took mankind from a "state of barbarism and the deepest misery to its present stage of civilization and well-being is the increasing understanding of the causal connection between things and human welfare, and increasing control of the less proximate conditions."[11] The correlation between knowledge and progress is a description of the nature of reality which

---
9   Ibid.
10 Ibid., 74
11 Ibid.

will continue to be true into the indefinite future, "Nothing is more certain than that the degree of economic progress of mankind will still, in future epochs, be commensurate with the degree of progress of human knowledge."[12]

Human flourishing and the development of our nature is bound to our understanding of the self and the world. Menger sees our needs as inherent in our nature; they have their origin in the distinctive composition of our being— "Needs arise from our drivers and the drivers are embedded in our nature."[13] The fulfillment of those desires (drivers) causes the satisfaction of our wants, it moves us from a state of uneasiness and unfulfillment to a state of satisfaction and contentment, i.e., happiness. On the contrary, "Failure to satisfy them [drivers] bring about our destruction"[14] or misery. "But to satisfy our needs is to live and prosper. Thus, attempting to provide for the satisfaction of our needs is synonymous with the attempt to provide for our lives and well-being."[15] Menger proceeds to make explicit the fundamental role that the fulfillment of our desires/needs entails for in it our happiness rests— "It is the most important of all human endeavors, since it is the prerequisite and foundation of all others."[16]

For Menger one can conclude that the source of wealth individually and collectively; including the degree of human development and the attainment of happiness is ultimately rooted in knowledge of the nature of reality. Knowledge is what is of most value since it provides access to the fulfillment of the needs embedded in our human nature. Hence, if happiness is to be attained, and if fulfillment and ever-increasing levels of civilization are to be achieved, then a proper metaphysical understanding of the nature of the self and the world is a necessary precondition.[17] Menger is seeking after a unified theory of human action which sets economics within the larger historical context of philosophy and ethics. If we as individuals and cultures are to flourish and attain our potential, then an engagement at the level of worldview and basic beliefs is the locus

---

12 Ibid.
13 Ibid., 77.
14 Ibid.
15 Ibid.
16 Ibid.
17 Menger, *Principles of Economics*, 53-54, 56, 72-73, 74, 77, 116, 120, 121, 128, 146-148.

of the discussion. The nature and causes of the wealth of nations reside primarily on the set of beliefs that render life intelligible and meaningful for the individuals that share a way of life that is true to reality.

It is important to note that the last five centuries have been in important illustration in the ascendancy of value. Collectively, the modern world had shifted in its assessment of value. Mercantilism sought conquest and precious metals; physiocratism looked for wealth in land; the industrial revolution shifted from natural resources to the mechanized processes to enhance the capabilities derived from raw materials; then the locus of progress moved from industry to technology by harvesting potentialities through new inventions. From technology we now live in the informational age where what is of value resides in the dispersion of information. Information is yet to attain to the next level, that is knowledge and wisdom regarding the understanding of the human person. Much progress has been attained in understanding the potential latent in the natural world (natural rule), but much progress remains to be uncovered regarding the human person and the need for wisdom. The progression between understanding, knowledge, and wisdom is the next stage of development in the ascendancy of valuation—the result of an objective value theory. Throughout this 500 year process the centrality of knowledge as understanding becomes clearer and most prominent in ascertaining what is of value. Menger pointed economists in the right direction, but he and his followers did not pursue further development in objective value theory. Next, we will explore how Ludwig von Mises was unable to develop objective value theory due to his commitment to Kantian epistemology and the denial of reason as ontological.

I. Mises' Praxiological Method: Limiting Economics to Subjective Value Theory

It is well known in the history of ideas that just as knowledge is gained, some knowledge is lost from generation to generation. In economics, the subjective value theory had been developed by the Spanish Scholastics in the High Middle Ages, then it was lost for a few centuries and finally rediscovered during the Marginalist Revolution led by Menger, Jevons, and Walras.[18] Menger's contribution to objective value theory may undergo a similar fate. While postulated and explained by Menger, it was left undeveloped and his most prominent heir in Austrian Economics, Ludwig von Mises, focused exclusively on subjective value. In this section I will explain how Mises' departure from Menger's objectivist theory of value led to a descriptive understanding of economics which limited economic analysis to the phenomenological dimension of human actions while neglecting the larger ethical framework to account for human action, cultural progress, human flourishing, and the attainment of real lasting happiness. According to Mises and subsequent Austrian Economists, economics is to be confined to the descriptive laws of human of human action and should abstain from making normative assessment of human conduct: "It is true that economics is a theoretical science and as such abstains from any judgement of value. It is not its task to tell people what ends they should aim at. It is a science of the means to be applied for the attainment of ends chosen, not, to be sure a science of the choosing of ends."[19] Mises thus confined economics to a science of means and not of ultimate ends. "Science never tells a man how he should act; it merely shows how a man must act if he wants to attain definitive ends."[20] In this same passage Mises proceeds to reject the objection raised by those like Menger who propose an objectivist theory of value—"It seems to people that this is very little indeed and that a science limited to the investigation of the *is* and unable to express a judgment of value about the highest and ultimate end is of no importance for life and action."[21] Mises narrows the science of economics to the descriptive realm and by implication becomes the advocate of skepticism in ethical questions regarding the purpose of human life. Murray N. Rothbard, Mises' closest disciple in the United States identified

---

18   Murray Rothbard in his history of economics—*Classical Economics: An Austrian Perspective on the History of Economic Thought*—places a considerable emphasis on the discovery and loss of knowledge in economic valuation. In addition, once can consult Marjorie Grice-Hutchinson's *Early Economic Thought in Spain, 1177-1740* where a historical account of the School of Salamanca is detailed.
19   Ludwig von Mises, *Human Action: A Treatise on Economics* (Auburn: Ludwig von Mises Institute, 1998), 10.
20   Ibid.
21   Ibid.

Mises departure from objective value theory as the most significant failure in Mises' economics:

> What I have been trying to say is that Mises's utilitarian, relativist approach to ethics is not nearly enough to establish a full case for liberty. It must be supplemented by an absolutist ethics—an ethics of liberty, as well as of other values needed for the health and development of the individual—grounded on natural law, i.e., discovery of the laws of man's nature. Failure to recognize this is the greatest flaw in Mises's philosophical worldview.[22]

The failure lies in abandoning the broader and more impactful aspect of life. If human action is purposeful behavior, and all actions have a highest end as their aim, and all intermediary actions become a means to the attainment of the ultimate end, the best way to improve human behavior is to define the end of human action and persuade our fellow human beings to align their personal, political, and economic actions in conformity with the supreme good. In other words, narrowing economics to understanding the praxeological implications of human choice in regard to policy does not affect the ultimate conception of the aim of human action. If one explains to a Buddhist or a dogmatic Marxist that their actions will not lead to greater utilitarian rewards, they both may be perfectly undisturbed by economic science since it does not align with the values established in their worldview. Public discourse over the concept of the good may have been a far broader subject to yield far greater and lasting outcomes. Economics has been circumscribed to means and not 'the *summum bonum*' as described by Mises himself: "Praxeology is indifferent to the ultimate goals of action. Its findings are valid for all kinds of action irrespective of the ends aimed at. It is a science of means, not ends."[23] Mises despaired on metaphysical inquiries regarding the nature of reality, he found them interminable and unanswerable: "There is no point in quarreling about these

---

22   Roberta Madugno, *Rothbard vs. The Philosophers: The Unpublished writings on Hayek, Mises, Strauss, and Polanyi*, (Auburn: Ludwig von Mises Institute, 2009), 112.
23   Mises, *Human Action*, 15.

problems [metaphysical]. Such metaphysical disputes are interminable. The present state of knowledge does not provide the means to solve them with an answer which every reasonable man must consider satisfactory."[24] Mises' skepticism of metaphysical inquiries closed the door to an objectivist account of human ends and its ethical dimension. This is a significant departure from Menger's distinction between 'real' and 'imaginary' goods. No longer can one speak of what ought to be the case objectively; one must limit inquiry to the subjective valuation of the individual actors in a coherentist approach without regard for truth. This is a costly price to pay in economics and in public discourse at large. If knowledge of ultimate ends is not possible, then conventional relativism either of the individual or the collective kind will prevail. Mises would have been greater served by continuing in the Mengerian tradition by searching after the indubitable foundations of objectivist claims to answer the most basic questions regarding the end of human action. Mises should have recognized the unavoidable nature of value judgments in human action and should have strived to attain further consensus in that direction rather than resting content with the underlying skepticism that led him to a pragmatic utilitarianism and the narrowing of economics to subjective value theory. The economist Wilhelm Ropke made the point that value judgments are ultimately inescapable in economics: "Science—above all, moral sciences of which economics is a part—is indeed inseparably mixed up with value judgments, and our efforts to eliminate them will only end in absurdity. If we look properly it is not difficult in economics to discover a value judgment lurking behind theories and propositions which give the outward appearance of innocent neutrality."[25] Yet Mises mistakenly believed that Praxeology had escaped having to account for objective value theory and that by confining itself to subjectivity it enabled it indifference to ethical considerations: "Because [praxeology] is subjectivistic and takes the value judgements of acting man as ultimate data not open to any further critical examination, it is itself above all strife of parties and factions, it is indifferent to the conflicts of all schools of dogmatism and ethical doctrines, it is free from valuations and preconceived ideas and judgements, it

---

24   Ludwig von Mises, *The Ultimate Foundation of Economic Science: An Essay on Method*, (Indiana: Liberty Fund, Inc., 2006), 6.
25   Wilhelm Ropke, *A Value Judgment on Value Judgments*, (Grand Rapids: Journal of Markets and Morality Vol. 18, Number 2, 2015), 504.

is universally valid and absolutely and plainly human."[26] In spite of Mises' intentions of bypassing considerations about objective value theory and contending views of value, his project left the economics incomplete in a normative sense. Much of the work that has been done in economics since Mises' contributions to the field have been in formulating a larger framework whereby economics can be tied to a more comprehensive understanding of the world. Friedrich Von Hayek (*The Constitution of Liberty*), Murray N. Rothbard (*The Ethics of Liberty*), Lew Rockwell (*Against the State: An Anarcho-Capitalist Manifesto*), and other Austrian Economists have ventured into this project without a satisfactory resolution.[27] The field of economics finds itself engulfed in philosophical, cultural, and ethical disputes without being able to provide a response. Three centuries of apologetical work in defense of the free market by pointing at the material benefits have not abated the cry for justice and equality by Socialists, Communists, and the forgotten members of society. If economics is to make progress in addressing value judgments, a revision of objective value theory rooted in philosophical, ethical, and worldview considerations is required. When the whole edifice is being challenged, one can only salvage it by developing a firmer foundation on which it stands. Until then, we should expect the slow, gradual, and contentious pattern of conflict and disputes that have brought public discourse to an impasse.

II. Conclusion: Menger's Objectivist Grounds for Economics based on Metaphysics

Carl Menger's objectivist theory of knowledge began a discourse that should be continued. In a century and a half since he wrote his *Principles of Economics* the need for objective value theory in public discourse has become all the more necessary. The disputes among different worldviews and cultures when engaged on the topic of political economy has increased the contention and perspectives given systematic disagreements regarding basic questions in metaphys-

---

26 Mises, *Human Action*, 21.
27 Only Austrian authors are mentioned for neither Keynesians nor Monetarists had any interest to explore the ethical, ontological, and metaphysical beliefs surrounding economics.

ics and ethics. The Mengerian postulation of objective value theory would have aided in understanding the source of the wealth of nations, rather than limiting the analysis of wealth to the division of labor or capital and investment, Menger's objective value theory would engage larger aspects of human nature and the nature of the world. Specifically, the role of beliefs and values in developing talent in human beings and establishing the purpose of uncovering the nature of things. This view of wealth connected with understanding the nature of reality would lay the foundation for unlimited wealth and fullness of life for generations without end. Rule over the self and over the world would unlock untapped potential in human culture, poverty springs primarily from ignorance and erroneous understanding of the world. Those countries and peoples of the world that have attained a view of reality for the self and the world have attained the highest levels of progress—the privilege of knowledge led them to name (understand the essence of things) and rule (develop things according to their natures) to increase the wealth of knowledge to improve the wellbeing of all involved. As described by the Philosopher Surrendra Gangadean: "The use of talent for the good increases the richness of life for all. Richness is proportional to fullness understood in its unity. This richness is fulfilling and inexhaustible and transformative. The more it is sought and shared, the more it increases in each person and for all persons. This richness is not separable from persons, but is experienced in and through all persons that seek the good."[28] It is this sense in which understanding leads to wealth that is comprehensive of all areas of life beyond the narrow confines of materialistic valuations which disregard the need for meaning and fulfillment in human beings.

---

28   Surrendra Gangadean, *Philosophical Foundation: A Critical Analysis of Basic Beliefs*, (Lanham: University Press of America, 2008), 193.

Bibliography

Gangadean, Surrendra. *Philosophical Foundation: A Critical Analysis of Basic Beliefs.* New York: University Press of America, 2008.

Hulsmann, Jorg Guido. *Mises: The Last Knight of Liberalism.* Auburn: Ludwig von Mises Institute, 2007.

Madugno, Roberta. *Rothbard vs. The Philosophers: The Unpublished writings on Hayek, Mises, Strauss, and Polanyi.* Auburn: Ludwig von Mises Institute, 2009.

Mises, Ludwig von. *Human Action: A Treatise on Economics.* Auburn: Ludwig von Mises Institute, 2008.

Mises, Ludwig von. *The Ultimate Foundation of Economic Science: An Essay on Method.* Indianapolis: Liberty Fund Inc., 2006.

Rothbard, Murray. *Classical Economics: An Austrian Perspective on the History of Economic Thought.* Auburn, Ludwig von Mises Institute, 1995.

Wilhelm Ropke, "A Value Judgment on Value Judgment," *Journal of Markets & Morality,* Vol. 18, no. 2 (2015): 497-517.

The Contemporary Free Will Solution: Is There Anything New?

Owen Anderson, Ph.D.
And
Matthew Nolen, Ph.D.

The problem of evil is a perennial problem that transcends academic philosophy and is especially felt in the lives of individuals as they struggle to make sense of their experiences. Epicurus famously stated the problem: Is God willing to prevent evil but not able? Then he is impotent. Is he able but not willing? Then he is malevolent. Is he both able and willing? Whence then is evil? The past few decades have seen a flourishing of Christians working in philosophy, what some (like George Marsden) call a renaissance of Christian thought. During this time possible solutions to the problem emerged, the most popular being the free will defense. This argument, if held consistently, relies on views that limit God's foreknowledge, a libertarian concept of the free will, and an analysis of what counts as the best of all possible worlds; nevertheless, this solution appeals to Christian in many different theological camps.

And yet, the astute critic will point out that neither this view of God's foreknowledge nor libertarian free will are new to the problem of evil debate. Indeed, what is presented in this defense was developed first by the Jesuit priest Luis de Molina in the 16th century. In itself, this is not surprising or a problem, but it raises the question of whether this solution really does successfully deal with the challenges that have arisen since the 16th century. Furthermore, the nuanced student of theology may point out that this formulation of God's foreknowledge was rejected by theologians like John Calvin, and needless to say, this view of freedom has also been rejected (and not just by Calvin, but by others such as Augustine and Jonathan Edwards). The rejection of libertarianism is not because of a rejection of freedom, but because of an Augustinian tradition about the will where freedom is consistent with predetermination due to a distinction between *want* and *ability*.

Where does that leave the contemporary discussion about the problem of evil? Are old solutions being recycled in the costume of current terminology? Are these old solutions acceptable again because of new insights, or because of unnoticed presuppositions? In the following, we will argue that David Hume, in his *Dialogues Concerning Natural Religion*, identified five common solutions to the problem of evil (through his three characters) and articulated the weakness for each.[1] Furthermore, the free will defense and the revival of Molinism fit into his categories so that if these are to be revised, they must successfully address the challenges Hume raised, particularly the fideism of his character Demea, and the anthropomorphism of his character Cleanthes. It will be contended that this defense has not adequately addressed Hume's critique. Particularly, this form of defense does not assist nonbelievers with belief; rather it only assists with those already committed to a particular system of belief. By way of contrast, solutions to the problem of evil require identifying the good in order to explain how evil can serve the good. It will be argued that an outline for a solution can be found in the Westminster Confession of Faith in a way that explains God's purpose in creation and providence, that preserves the freedom and dignity of the human will, anticipates the challenges given voice by Hume, and yet does not neatly fit into contemporary solutions because these solutions are based on limiting presuppositions about the goal of the Christian life.

Although our research is informed by notable advocates of the free will defense, we are studying this defense in a generic form to argue that this was anticipated by Hume. Here are some features that help identify the way this defense is formulated:

1. This approach distinguishes between a defense and a theodicy; a defense is sufficient to show that belief in God is not

---

[1] Hume, D., & Smith, N. K. (1935). Hume's dialogues concerning natural religion. Oxford: Clarendon Press.

2. These approaches argued that there is not a contradiction in the classic statement of the problem of evil.
3. The apparent contradiction is resolved by noting that it is not clearly the case that an all good and all-powerful being would create a world without evil because the existence of evil might be consistent with a greater good.
4. This defense only requires resolving the apparent contradiction and positing that "for all we know there is a greater good."
5. In analyzing which possible world to actualize, those using this defense say God picks the world with the greatest good and least amount of evil, which requires:
    a. Persons with libertarian free will that can freely choose to do evil
    b. The incarnation of the Son of God and his death to demonstrate love
    c. Other kinds of goodness such as beauty, justice, love of neighbor, etc.
6. Indeed, the greatest good is this incarnation and death. Thus, a supralapsarian system is relied upon where God created a world that would include this, and consequently also had to create a world that included the evil that necessitated this.
7. This defense claims that the best of all possible worlds is one that includes God and includes the incarnation/atonement, and the amount of evil is a matter for the goodness of God that we cannot understand.

The Historical Context of the Problem

Historically Hume's skepticism can be credited with initiating the decline of natural theology. Kant tried to respond to Hume but agreed that pure reason and the traditional theistic proofs are ineffectual. Instead, Kant placed the question of God's existence in the realm of practical rationality. Following this lead, theologians like Schleiermacher and anthropologists like Rudolph Otto argued for the ground of religiosity in the sense or experience of the divine/

holy. The 19th century seemed to add nail after nail to the coffin of natural theology, whether through Darwin's reliance on evil and suffering in his theory of origins, or Lessing's Ditch, or Strauss's higher criticism, thus, having no need for God, the century ended with Nietzsche's declaration about God's death.

The 19th and early 20th centuries saw an increase of unbelief among intellectuals. On one level this was due to an increase in naturalistic explanations that relied on the assumption that only the material world exists. However, for this view to have credence, it was coupled with the claim that there are no successful theistic arguments, and that God could not exist given all of the evil in the world (both natural and moral evil). This is essentially how Hume presented the condition of theism in *Dialogues Concerning Natural Religion*, and little has changed in the presentation of more recent critics like J.L. Mackie. As thinkers like Alvin Plantinga finished their graduate work and began careers in philosophy, the atmosphere was heavily saturated with atheism so that a theist would be viewed as holding a belief that was rationally suspect if not altogether absurd. Out of this atmosphere, the theistic renaissance emerged and was compelled to answer the claim of irrationality in light of the problem of evil.

Before going further in the analysis of contemporary solutions, it will be profitable to consider how the problem of evil was understood by skeptics and presented to the new generation of Christian philosophers. What solutions have been anticipated before this generation? As a summary work that answers this question, we will look at Hume's *Dialogues Concerning Natural Religion*. Indeed, we will find little that was not anticipated by Hume explicitly or by implication in contemporary theists or atheists.

Hume, in his dialogic format, presented five solutions and had his character Philo indicate the problems in each. Philo ends by affirming skepticism about the human ability to find a solution, and this continues to be the default position for both theist and atheist. The five solutions are nested in Hume's larger belief that no evil is necessary. He says: "Now, this I assert to be the case with regard to all the causes of evil, and the circumstances, on which it depends. None of them appear to human reason, in the least degree, necessary or unavoidable; nor can we suppose them such, without utmost license of imagination."[2]

Contemporary thinkers such as Markham and Pike, like the character Philo, argue that there could have been less evil.[3] Echoing Hume, "that pain or misery in man is *compatible* with infinite power and goodness in the deity,"[4] They claim a solution might be possible, yet it has not been discovered. As Hume makes known, along with Markham, Pike and Rowe,[5] If one begins with the presupposition that God exists the problem of evil will not likely detract one from that position; however, if one does not begin with the preconceived notion of God's existence then evil would likely stop one from coming to belief in a perfect deity. Hume captures this by saying that if a stranger were to drop into this world, he would conclude that evil far out-shadows good.[6] By revisiting Hume's five responses to the problem of evil it will be seen that modern theodicies have not taken the argument beyond Hume. In existing literature, theodicies can be understood as a mixture of these five responses, though most will generally be understood as an appeal to the unknown.

The World Is Full of Misery and Wickedness—More Good Than Evil?

Hume begins by arguing that the world is full of misery and wickedness. The character Cleanthes tries to reject this by asserting that "the only method of supporting Divine benevolence, (and it is what I willingly embrace,) is to deny absolutely the misery and wickedness of man."[7] Philo responds in two ways, first by saying that such a claim is contrary to everyone's experience, "it is contrary to an authority so established as nothing can subvert: No decisive proofs can ever be produced against this authority; nor is it possible

---

2   Ibid., 252.
3   Pike, Nelson. "Hume on Evil." The Philosophical Review 72, no. 2 (1963): 180-197.; Markham, Ian. «Hume Revisited: A Problem with the Free Will Defense." Modern Theology 7, no. 3 (1991): 281-290.
4   Smith, 248.
5   Rowe, William L. "The Problem of Evil and Some Varieties of Atheism." American Philosophical Quarterly 16, no. 4 (1979): 335-341.
6   Smith, 241.
7   Ibid., 246.

for you to compute, estimate, and compare, all the pains and all the pleasures in the lives of all men and of all animals: And thus, by your resting the whole system of religion on one point, which, from its very nature, must forever be uncertain, you tacitly confess, that that system is equally uncertain."[8]

Hume also beings his polemic against theism by asking, "why is there any misery at all in the world?" Indeed, Philo says that even if he grants that the misery and wickedness of the world are compatible with divine power and goodness, this does not prove that the present mixed and confused phenomena proceed from God and God alone.[9] Furthermore, misery and wickedness are not necessary and could be easily avoided if God is all good and powerful.

God is Finite in Power

Cleanthes responds by arguing for *anthropomorphism* where God is understood to be essentially like humans, although perhaps greater in power. This is very like the way that Molinists argue about God's foreknowledge, casting it as the same kind of decision-making process found in finite humans. God, for the Molinists, is not the determiner but the foreknower where the latter means he looks into the future to learn his options rather than determining them by creating the nature of things. Philo replies that even a limited, finite being could create a world better than this one. "In short, I repeat the question: Is the world, considered in general, and as it appears to us in this life, different from what a man or such a limited being would, *beforehand*, expect from a very powerful, wise, and benevolent Deity? It must be strange prejudice to assert the contrary."[10]

The Free Will solution, and its reliance on middle knowledge, limits what God knows and what God can do, his wisdom and power. Indeed, advocates of this theory often take the time to argue for a definition of "omnipotence" that allows that term to be applied to a limited being so that they do not appear to be abandoning theism. However, theism differs from Aristotelian dualism (a view closer to

8   Ibid., 247.
9   Ibid., 248.
10 Ibid., 251.

what Molinists mean by "God"); in theism, God is the creator not simply the one who actualizes potentialities. God as the creator and infinite in wisdom necessarily determines the nature, will, and condition of his creation in any and all possible worlds. The limitation placed upon God's wisdom and power is, therefore, counter to the theistic cosmology of creation *ex nihilo;* the implication being, God according to his nature created all other states of affair. The denial of this leads into suppositions, such that, God did not actualize the

state of affairs consisting in the existence of 'necessary states of affairs.'[11]

We Will Know in the Afterlife

Demea argues that it is beyond human capacity to know the answer to such problems in this life; therefore, our only hope is to learn the answer in the next life. Demea posits that "the present evil phenomena, therefore, are rectified in other regions, and in some future period of existence. And the eyes of men, being then opened to larger views of things, see the whole connection of general laws, and trace, with adoration, the benevolence and rectitude of the Deity, through all the mazes and intricacies of his providence."[12] Furthermore, Hume responded to the popular analogous claim made by theodicies that, when viewing life in retrospect in the felicitous beatific vision all suffering will be viewed as sufficiently good.[13] This claim is often used to appeal to a skeptical understanding of the nature of man and/or God. While attempting to maintain God's nature, the theodicy appeals to a future state of being, in which the believer will understand, "from the post-mortem perspective of the beatific vision, such suffering will be seen for what they were, and retrospectively no one will wish away any intimate encounters with God from his/her life-history in this world."[14] Hume's polemical re-

---

11   Plantinga, Alvin. The nature of necessity. Oxford University Press on Demand, 1978.
12   Smith, 245.
13   Adams, Marilyn McCord, and Stewart Sutherland. "Horrendous Evils and the Goodness of God." Proceedings of the Aristotelian Society, Supplementary Volumes 63 (1989): 297-323.
14   Ibid., 219.

sponse to this position is to say, "to establish one hypothesis upon another is building entirely in the air; and the utmost we ever attain, by these conjecture and fictions, is to ascertain the bare possibility of our opinion; but never can we, upon such terms, establish its reality."[15] Thus, the believer is still not rationally justified nor is unbeliever held culpable due to the lack of justification.

God is Incomprehensible

Another solution considered by Hume is that God's goodness is incomprehensible, and we must trust that he loves us. Love is a virtue. Virtues are not ends in themselves but obtained for the sake of something else. Therefore, virtues are a means to the good, not the good itself. Further explanation of the good is required from theodicies to show how suffering is indeed an act of love. To love another is to seek the good for him/her. Therefore, the good needs to be defined and evil demands justification towards that end. To avoid the answer, scholars appeal to a limitation upon cognitive faculties. Love for a creature could require it suffering to a certain extent, however, as Hume, as well as Markham and Pike, that there could be less evil, and if we cannot know the goodness of God then all praise and prayer ends.

Along with these theodicies is often a skeptical disclaimer such as, "as theologians we have nothing to say definitively about the nature of God and should therefore more often standing in silence before the Holy Mystery."[16] Or again, "If we realize the magnitude of the theistic proposal, cognizance of suffering thus should not in the least reduce our confidence that it is true."[17] These skeptical disclaimers suppose that cognitive faculties of the finite can never wholly understand the nature of the infinite; this is true in part. The finite cannot *completely* understand the infinite, yet one expects as they grow,

---

15 Smith, 245.
16 Putz, Oliver. "Love Actually: A Theodicy Response to Suffering in Nature. In Dialogue with Francisco Ayala." Theology and Science 7, no. 4 (2009): 345-361, 358.
17 Wykstra, Stephen J. "The Humean Obstacle to Evidential Arguments from Suffering: On Avoiding the Evils of "Appearance"." International Journal for Philosophy of Religion16, no. 2 (1984): 73-93.

even slowly, to in time increase in understanding. Though disclaimers go as far as to say that the finite can never understand *any* of the infinite. Undoubtedly, Hume preempted these conjectures, "a mere possible compatibility is not sufficient. You must *prove* these, pure, unmixed, and uncontrollable attributes from the present mixed and confused phenomena, and from these alone."[18] If unbelief is culpable then, objective proof is necessary, yet insufficient subjective proofs has been given in response to the problem of evil.

More Good than Evil Exists, and Natural Evil is not Necessary

Solutions to the problem of evil distinguish between natural and moral evils. Often, the former is taken for granted as a feature of the world. However, Hume argues that no natural evil is necessary, and suggests four conditions that, if different, would greatly improve life. These are: no pain is necessary, secret divine intervention could greatly increase the good in the world without overriding natural laws, greater natural diligence and attention to details of the world, and the excesses of nature are not necessary. In present scholarship, none have attempted to explicate the purpose of natural evil while being able to maintain God's infinite nature, a compatibilist view of evil. This requires, to be consistent with infinite wisdom, that there be a necessary, knowable, good brought through this evil.

A common solution supposed by modern theodicies that Hume considers in this larger context is that such evils are necessary to produce a virtuous person. Appeals to soul/person making are attempts to show that more good than evil exists, either in a future or present state, and that natural evil is not necessary. According to Hick and Adams, the idea of person/soul-making is based upon the supposition that to understand/appreciate good one must experience evil, the greater the suffering, the greater the appreciation.[19]

18 Smith, 248.
19 John Hick, 'Soul-Making and Suffering', in Adams and Adams, eds. The Problem of Evil, pp. 168–188. Reprinted from John Hick, Evil and The God of Love, rev. edn. (New York: Harper and Row, 1978), pp. 255–265, 318–336; Adams, R. M. (1977). "Middle Knowledge and the Problem of Evil." American Philosophical Quarterly, 14(2), 109-117.

For courage to exist or have meaning danger must exist. Hick holds that the current state of evil is appropriate to cause soul-making, yet it fails as much as it succeeds in this world. The defense of this position is, "If we must compare two virtual infinites, we can only say that the sum of contentment and happiness is greater than the sum of misery, since otherwise mankind would long since have destroyed itself."[20] Yet, Hume notes that "it is hard; I dare to repeat it, it is hard, that being placed in a world so full of wants and necessities; where almost every being and element is either our foe or refuses its assistance; we should also have our own temper to struggle with, and should be deprived of that faculty, which can alone fence against these multiplied evils."[21] We need virtue precisely to deal with natural evils and the wickedness of others. Therefore, to argue that evil is present to teach us virtue is a circular argument.

God is Indifferent

From these considerations, Philo concludes that God is indifferent. "The whole presents nothing but the idea of a blind nature, impregnated by a great vivifying principle, and pouring forth from her lap, without discernment or parental care, her maimed and abortive children."[22] Therefore, the original source of all things must be entirely indifferent to our condition.[23] Modern responses from both Corabi and Putz[24] Rely on intelligent design and theistic evolution have presupposed this notion that Philo deduced. Hume concludes that God if he exists, is indifferent to his creation. Both theories are subject to this critique in that they assume within original creation that NE was present. This is inconsistent with the Biblical account of Genesis 1-3, and therefore can be rejected in a theodicy for theistic beliefs that hold to scripture.

---

20 Hick, 177.
21 Smith, 257.
22 Ibid., 260.
23 Ibid., 260.
24 Corabi, Joseph. "Intelligent Design and Theodicy." Religious Studies 45, no. 1 (2009): 21-35; Putz.

Hume Anticipated the Free Will Defense

The Free Will defense of contemporary philosophers is simply a restatement of solutions considered by Hume in the characters of Demea and Cleanthes. It asserts that God is limited in what he can do (a finite deity) and that for all we know there is a good that makes sense of the evil (all will be revealed in a future state). Such defenses will only be as a strong as their assumptions, and Hume had a skill in identifying assumptions. Although Hume did not consider, in the *Dialogues*, the problem with libertarian free will he does demonstrate this elsewhere.

Assuming the reality of causation, and God's existence, libertarian free will has been rejected. Concurrently, contemporary philosophers raise questions about libertarian free will not being possible or likely.[25] For libertarian free will to be a reality, freedom would be utter randomness or uncaused events. Determinism, the opposite of libertarian freewill, hard or soft, has also been seen as not being possible. Reichenbach charged compatibilists, exemplified in the Westminster Confession, to rationally justifying the good brought from the redemption of mankind, which was necessitated by the Fall.[26] Reichenbach denies the original Fall of man due to scientific discoveries and finds compatibilism unjustifiable. If the free will defense can account for a certain amount of evil due to man's free will (moral evil), there is still the evil that is not accounted for by the human will, natural evil.[27] In an attempt to account for evil outside of human free will Plantinga appeals to Satan's free will.[28] Such an

---

[25] Van Inwagen, Peter. "The Problem of Evil: The Gifford Lectures Delivered in the University of Saint Andrews in 2003." (2006); Mackie, John L. "Evil and omnipotence." Mind 64, no. 254 (1955): 200-212; Trakakis, Nick. «Theodicy: The Solution to the Problem of Evil, or Part of the Problem?." Sophia 47, no. 2 (2008): 161.

[26] Reichenbach, Bruce R. "Evil and a Reformed view of God." International journal for philosophy of religion (1988): 67-85.

[27] O'Connor, David. "A Reformed Problem of Evil and the Free Will Defense." International journal for philosophy of religion 39, no. 1 (1996): 33-63, 48; van Inwagen, 83; Grant, Stephen. «Evil And Possible Worlds.» (2006); Mackie; Adams, Marilyn McCord, and Stewart Sutherland. «Horrendous Evils and the Goodness of God." Proceedings of the Aristotelian Society, Supplementary Volumes 63 (1989): 297-323.

[28] Plantinga, Alvin. "Supralapsarianism, or 'O Felix Culpa'." An Antholo-

attempt simply pushes back the question (why God has allowed evil in the first place) and does not give an account for evil because in theism Satan is a result of God's creation, and his actions are according to God's providence.

To give an account of evil Mackie, van Inwagen, and Judisch[29] Have argued that one is truly free if their will is uncaused, therefore, by necessary consequences God must be finite in power. This is not dissimilar to libertarian free will and leaves libertarians in a difficult place, defending uncaused events and a finite deity. In theism, the nature of man should be viewed in light of the nature of God; finite in light of the infinite. A given thinker's view of free will reveals more basic presuppositions, consistent or inconsistent with the nature of God. Given causation, only a compatibilist view of free will and God can answer the problem of evil.

Contemporary Solutions

In 1955, J.L. Mackie published *Evil and Omnipotence* which argues that for a theist to solve the problem of evil, one of the premises in the problem must be given up. That is, either God is not perfect in goodness or not perfect in power. Epicurus anticipated this in his statement of the problem, and more recently Hume had considered these possible solutions. In a brilliant rhetorical style, Hume maneuvered through five attempted solutions and their deficiencies, as well as demonstrating that no natural evil is necessary.

Like Hume before him, Mackie restated the problem of evil: one must either say God is not infinite in power or in goodness to solve the problem of evil. Epicurus said: "is God's will to prevent evil, but not able? Then he is not omnipotent. Is he able but not willing? Then he is malevolent. Is he both able and willing? Then whence cometh evil? Is he neither able nor willing? Then why call him God?" Mackie, like Hume, argued that the only solution a theist will

---

gy (2004)

29 Judisch, Neal. "Theological Determinism and the Problem of Evil." Religious Studies 44, no. 2 (2008): 165-184.

find is to either deny that God is all powerful or deny that God is all good. Indeed, we will see that this is precisely the path taken by subsequent theists in responding to this problem.

The Free Will Defense

Alvin Plantinga's free will defense challenged Mackie's claims and reinvigorated the philosophy of religion among Christians.[30] Plantinga distinguished between a defense that diffuses the problem of evil and takes away its force as an objection to belief in God, and a theodicy which explains why there is evil in light of the power and goodness of God. His stated purpose is the former, to show that there is not an actual contradiction in the claims that God is all good, all powerful, and evil exists.

Alvin Plantinga's work in this area began as a response to Mackie's claims about the problem of evil and omnipotence. Plantinga argued that there is not really a contradiction between the statements that God is all good and all powerful and yet evil exists.[31] This is because evil might serve some higher good that God wants to instantiate, but which cannot be instantiated with some instances of evil. Plantinga does name some possible contenders, such as love, character growth, and relationships, he says that it is sufficient to say that for all we know there is such a good, and if God exists, we can trust that there is indeed such a good. According to Plantinga, this defense is sufficient to show that the problem of evil is not a threat to the warrant of theistic belief.

In response scholars such as Grant, Markham, Pike, and Mackie ask, why this greater good cannot be achieved apart from evil. To deal with this objection, Plantinga developed his free will defense.[32] In this, he was essentially reaching back to Molina from the 17th century. This defense says that to have loving relationships humans need free will. Free will means that the will is undetermined, and that God cannot create a world in which free beings always choose

---

30 Stackhouse, Jr JG. "Mind Over Skepticism." Christianity Today 45, no. 8 (2001): 74-76.
31 Plantinga, 1974, 2004, and 2009.
32 Plantinga, 1974.

what is good. Therefore, this world is the best possible world that contains free beings.

Plantinga also analyzed the concept of omnipotence and argued that God can be omnipotent and yet some instances of evil be outside the control of God because of human free will.[33] Obviously, this requires a counter-causal, or libertarian, view of free will. This view of freedom is intimately tied to God's nature, foreknowledge, and purpose in creating. God considers all logically possible worlds and instantiates the one that has the maximal good with the least evil. According to Plantinga,[34] this is a world that includes God, includes humans with free will, includes the incarnation, atoning death, and resurrection of Christ, along with various virtues like love, kindness, empathy, courage, etc.

This view of God requires that God does not predetermine by creating but by choosing the possible world that most closely fits his will. That world may include many things that God does not will individually, but because the world taken as a whole is the best option before God, he chooses that world. According to Plantinga, the main point of God's will is that his love should be displayed to humanity through the incarnation and atonement.[35] This display of love is the higher good that makes some evil permissible.

In presenting the atonement this way, Plantinga is a supralapsarian. That is, before the Fall of humanity had even occurred, God had predetermined the incarnation and the election of some of humanity. This is in contrast to infralapsarianism that states that there is an order in God's eternal degree, from Creation, to Fall, to Redemption. One criticism of infralapsarianism is that this could be taken to imply that God is changing his plan as human events unfold (i.e., the Fall). However, as Charles Hodge pointed out in his *Systematic Theology*, infralapsarianism should not be taken this way but instead should be taken as recognizing the logical (although timeless) order between the Fall and Redemption.

Consequently, for Plantinga, the goal of God's act of creation is to demonstrate his love through the incarnation and atonement.[36] By

---

[33] Plantinga, 2004 and 2009.
[34] Plantinga, 2004.
[35] Ibid., 2004.
[36] Ibid.

way of contrast, the Reformed Tradition, summarized in the Westminster Standards, says that the purpose of God in creating is to manifest the glory of his wisdom, power, justice, goodness, and mercy. That is, there is much more to this revelation than the love of God in the incarnation and atonement, and this narrow focus misses the revelation of attributes of God such as his justice. The result is that natural evil is downplayed or attributed to the free will of other beings,[37] rather than to the justice and mercy of God as imposed after the Fall in Genesis 3. We will consider some problems that arise in contemporary solutions that narrow the purpose of God to this view of love.

There is a real sense in which no contemporary solution was unanticipated by Hume. He anticipated the Free Will Solution in his discussion that no natural evil is necessary. He anticipated solutions that say we cannot know why evil happens, or that for all we know there is a greater good, or we must wait until the afterlife, or God is doing his best, or our definition of 'good' is not the same as God's definition of 'good.' As far as the rhetoric of the situation goes, some persons are committed to theism and others to non-theism, and they give arguments based on this prior commitment. Some of these persons are more or less eloquent or influential, and their arguments garner attention based on these kinds of factors even if they do not express anything new or not already addressed by Hume.

Defining the Good

But if one has not already made up one's mind, or is engaged in leading the examined life and willing to question presuppositions, what does this say about the state of belief in God? Plantinga gives us a story about God wanting to express his love and picking a possible world that best allows this to happen. Why should we believe this story? The problem is predicated upon God's existence. And yet, the problem of evil is itself a challenge to the possibility of God's existence. The solution seems to depend upon what is meant by *God*, and particularly what is meant by the *goodness* of God. When

---

37   Ibid.

Plantinga says that for all we know there is a higher good that is served, we must be able to define the term *good* to make sense of this claim. A deeper definition of the good will help solve the problem of evil and help explain the relationship between unbelief, the Fall, and the need for redemption within the larger context of God's creating to reveal his glory.

In the case of Plantinga's solution, he identifies various goods (soul-making, the resurrection, fellowship with Christ through suffering) that he believes require the existence of some forms of evil.[38] These tend to be virtues that require evil as an obstacle to be overcome to build character, prompt loving relationships, or demonstrates instances of courage and commitment. This includes the highest good of the incarnation and atonement which would not be necessary if there was not evil to be atoned for. A similar solution has been advanced by John Hick which says that evil is necessary for soul-making, for learning to be virtuous and building character. The claim is that such virtues as love would not be possible or not as deep in a world without evil. Like Plantinga, Hick believes that the death of Christ can be understood as an example of love that leads others to live lives of selflessness. However, Hick does not believe that Christ is God incarnate or that his death is an atoning sacrifice. Should we follow Hick or Plantinga?

The Good

What the difference between Hick and Plantinga elucidates is that Christ can be appealed to as an example of love by persons with drastically different conceptions of what it means for him to be an example of love and with radically different conceptions of the nature of God and Christ. In other words, to appeal to Christ as an example of love is insufficient to establish the truth or even coherence of a story such as Plantinga presents. What must be done is to show that God exists and has a specific nature, and then to connect the person and work of Christ to this larger understanding of who God is. Furthermore, since both Plantinga and Hick agree that Christ is in some sense a response to evil, that term must be more clearly

---

38 Ibid.

defined to understand in what sense Christ reveals love.

The *goods* that proponents of the free will defense name as justifying evil are *virtues* rather than *ends*. For instance, love is the act of seeking the good for another and so cannot itself be the good. Similarly, in friendship we seek the good together, and so friendship cannot be the good. Both love and friendship presuppose that those involved know what is good (I cannot seek the good for you if I do not know what it is). The same is true of other virtues like kindness, temperance, hope, empathy; these are necessary as a means to an end. Furthermore, in many cases, these are necessary to persevere and overcome evil, and therefore it becomes circular to say that evil is necessary to build character (instill these virtues), and we need these virtues to overcome evil.

The means/end relationship between virtues and the end in itself is not a form of consequentialism. In consequentialism, the end in itself is confused with the effect of possessing the end in itself (happiness). Therefore, to argue that God would create the world in which the most people would be happy is to say that God would create the world in which the good is most fully instantiated. But this is precisely the non-theist's objection, that this world is not such a world. To try and get around this problem without actually giving a definition of *the good* that is most fully instantiated, and which is increased by evil is to beg the question.

The Good in Creation

Behind the non-theist's statement of the problem of evil is an intuition that the world should be free of evil if God exists and is all good and all powerful. The non-theist argues from the actuality of evil to the non-existence of God. However, the theist can reverse this argument, and argue that since God exists the original creation must have been very good (without evil). That is, the reality of evil now does not imply that there has always been evil. It may indeed have been the case that God created a world without evil and that some time after the original creation something happened which brought evil into the world, and that this event was permitted by the divine providence as a means of deepening the revelation of the good. It follows by necessity that if God is infinitely good and infinitely powerful, then he would and could have created a world without evil in it. To understand how a change occurred requires knowing what is the good in order to understand how the good can be deepened.

The Good Based Upon the Nature of a Being

Assuming a theistic context for a moment, good and evil for humanity are based on human nature, which is determined by God. This is simply to say that what is good for a being depends on the nature of a being, and within theism, God as the creator of human nature is the determiner of good and evil for human nature. The free will defense maintains that free will is necessary for human dignity because it is necessary for choice. The capacity to understand is more basic than free will (for human dignity) because presupposed by free will is the capacity to understand (if one cannot understand one cannot exercise free will to make choices). The good for humans is rooted in understanding, and specifically in understanding the highest reality. Consider the denial of this, something like, "understanding is not that important for our humanity," it is asking us to understand—that is, the denial is self-referentially absurd. The highest good for humans is understanding the highest reality, or: the highest good for humans (in theism) is to know God (the highest reality).

If the highest good for humans is to know God, does evil hinder or deepen this knowledge? Distinguishing between moral evil and natural evil we can precede one at a time. If the good in theism is knowing God, then evil is unbelief. In theism, if unbelief is culpable, then it must be clear that God exists so that unbelief is without excuse. Therefore, unbelief reveals something about the human condition and about the nature of God in his response to unbelief. That is, the reality of unbelief deepens what can be known about the nature of God. The unbeliever who says, "I can't believe in God because of all the *evil* in the world" can be interpreted as saying "I can't believe in God because of all the *unbelief* in the world," and since speaker is one of the persons in the world, this can be rephrased as "I cannot believe in God because of all the *unbelief in me*." Hardly an indictment against God, this becomes a revelation of the justice of God in leaving persons to their hardness of heart.

Contemporary free will defense advocates often interpret natural evil as either punishment for moral evil or the result of free choices by personal beings. We can proceed by rejecting both of these. Natural evil cannot be divine punishment for moral evil because it is not inherent to moral evil. The inherent consequences of moral evil would be a failure to achieve the good and all that follows. Nor can natural evil be due to the free choice of created beings. If the original creation was very good, without evil, then the change from *no natural evil* to *natural evil* would be on the same order as creation. Created beings, whether human or angelic/demonic, cannot create in the sense of bringing being into being or reconstituting the natural world against God's plan.

Instead, natural evil is imposed on humans as a call back from moral evil. It is *imposed* because it is not *inherent*. According to infinite justice humans could have been left without natural evil in the state of moral evil. It is a call back from moral evil because the only proportional response of such a change to the natural condition of man would be a similarly dramatic change to the spiritual/moral condition of man. Thus, natural evil is a kind of natural sign of the moral condition of man. This is not to suggest that it is a one-to-one sign as if those who suffer greatly are in more need of a call back. Indeed, in the case of Job, this was reversed—he suffered greatly but was the most righteous. However, his suffering produced the final result that he repented of sin he found in himself and claimed to have come to see God in a greater way.

The world being plunged into natural evil is a natural sign of the world being plunged into moral evil. Therefore, natural evil does not threaten the existence of God but instead can be understood as a revelation of the mercy of God. Rather than leave humans to themselves in moral evil, God imposed natural evil on the world as a call back indicating God's intention to redeem a fallen humanity. For those who heed this call back, natural evil also serves to remove moral evil. The very object of the problem of evil is itself a reminder of the mercy and justice of God.

This is an alternative solution to the Free Will Defense due to the deficiencies of that view. The free will defense claims that the evil in the world is due to free will, and that free will is necessary for human dignity. This is a counter-causal free will that brings with it many problems about uncaused events. Apart from those, the free will defense does not specify what the good is which is deepened by evil. When adherents of this view do try to be specific, they generally name virtues or happiness, and not an end in itself. By way of contrast, we have argued that while free will is necessary for moral evil, it is not sufficient to explain why God would permit moral evil. To simply suggest that there is possibly a higher good is to beg the question, and this insufficiency was noted by Hume.[39]

We have also argued that Hume anticipated and defeated the common solutions still being offered today. Hume's own historical context (Scottish Reformed), and the fact that important proponents of free will defense come from the Reformed background make it worthwhile to consider how the Westminster Confession of Faith (WCF and catechisms) address this problem. Though Hume would have rejected the Shorter Catechism, given the climate at the time would have been familiar with it. The WCF stands as the last of the Reformed Creeds, synthesizing and building on what came before.

Chapter 3.1 of the Confession is about God's Eternal Decree. In that chapter it says: "God from all eternity, did, by the most wise and holy counsel of His own will, freely, and unchangeably ordain whatsoever comes to pass; yet so, as thereby neither is God the author of sin, nor is violence offered to the will of the creatures; nor is the liberty or contingency of second causes taken away, but rather established." This eternal degree is not the kind of foreknowledge presented in Molinism and by Plantinga. Indeed, the Confession says, "Although God knows whatsoever may or can come to pass upon all supposed conditions; yet has He not decreed anything because He foresaw it as future, or as that which would come to pass upon such conditions." Rather, God determines all that comes to pass for the manifestation of His glory (3.3).

The Fall of man is an event in human history that was determined by God for the revelation of his glory. "Our first parents, be-

---

39 Smith, 247.

ing seduced by the subtlety and temptations of Satan, sinned, in eating the forbidden fruit. This their sin, God was pleased, according to His wise and holy counsel, to permit, having purposed to order it to His own glory." (6.1) The Fall is a sin which requires free will, but the Confession affirms a compatibilist view of free will and rejects the idea Transworld-depravity: "God has endued the will of man with that natural liberty, that is neither forced, nor, by any absolute necessity of nature, determined good, or evil." (9.1) It is not the case that man sins in every possible world (is of necessity determined to evil).

However, man's will is both free and predetermined by God. This is true in each state of mankind: before the Fall, after the Fall but before redemption, after redemption but before glorification, and in the glorified state.

> II. Man, in his state of innocency, had freedom, and power to will and to do that which was good and well pleasing to God; but yet, mutably, so that he might fall from it
>
> III. Man, by his fall into a state of sin, has wholly lost all ability of will to any spiritual good accompanying salvation: so as, a natural man, being altogether averse from that good, and dead in sin, is not able, by his own strength, to convert himself, or to prepare himself thereunto.
>
> IV. When God converts a sinner, and translates him into the state of grace, He frees him from his natural bondage under sin; and, by His grace alone, enables him freely to will and to do that which is spiritually good; yet so, as that by reason of his remaining corruption, he does not perfectly, or only, will that which is good, but does also will that which is evil.
>
> V. The will of man is made perfectly and immutably free to do good alone in the state of glory only."

Therefore, while "the light of nature shows that there is a God, who has lordship and sovereignty over all, is good, and does good unto all, and is therefore to be feared, loved, praised, called upon, trusted in, and served, with all the heart, and with all the soul, and with all the might (21.1)," moral evil is the rejection of this knowledge of God. The predestination of man to unbelief is consistent with free will in that at every point humans are able to do what they want. The predestination of moral and natural evil is consistent with the nature of God because, as Plantinga points out, the premises of the problem of evil are not contradictions of there being a higher good that evil serves. The Confession identifies and explains what this good is, and the Shorter Catechism begins by teaching: The chief end of man is to glorify God and enjoy him forever. (1:1)

Conclusion

The contention here is that contemporary theists have not produced a response to the problem of evil that was unanticipated by past skeptics, most vehemently David Hume. The problem that Hume identified in the character Demea was a kind of fideism which postponed knowledge of the good until the future. Contemporary theists still tend to fall into this category, repeating the mistakes of Demea. The problem of evil rests on fideism about the good and about the existence of God. The problem is stated as a reason to not believe in God in response to arguments that attempt to show the plausibility of belief. If, however, God's existence is objectively clear to reason so that unbelief is without excuse, then the realty of moral evil and natural evil can be seen to serve the good of knowing God. Indeed, if it is the case that all of creation and history serve to reveal the nature of God, then it can be affirmed that for those who know the good, all things work together for the good. So, while solutions of later thinkers were anticipated by Hume, Hume's contentions were addressed by the still earlier work in the WCF.

Bibliography

Adams, M. M., & Sutherland, S. (1989). *Horrendous Evils and the Goodness of God.* The Aristotelian Society: Supplementary Volume, 63 297-323.

Adams, R. M. (1977). "Middle knowledge and The Problem of Evil". *American Philosophical Quarterly*, 14(2), 109-117.

Adams, M. M., & Adams, R. M. (1990). *The Problem of Evil.* Oxford; New York: Oxford University Press.

Corabi, J. (2009). "Intelligent Design and Theodicy". *Religious Studies: An International Journal for the Philosophy of Religion*, 45(1), 21-35.

Grant, S. (2006). "Evil and Possible Worlds". *Philosophical Writings*, 31, 3.

Hick, J. (1966). *Soul-making and Suffering. Evil and The God of Love* (pp. 255-61-318-36). San Francisco: Harper & Row.

Hume, D., & Smith, N. K. (1935). *Hume's Dialogues Concerning Natural Religion.* Oxford: Clarendon Press.

Mackie, J. L. (1955). "Evil and Omnipotence". *Mind*, 64(254), 200-212.

Markham, Ian. "Hume Revisited: A Problem With The Free Will Defense." *Modern Theology* 7, no. 3 (1991): 281-290.

McCord Adams, M. (1989). "Horrendous Evils and The goodness of God". *Proceedings of the Aristotelian Society*, 297–310.

Nelson Pike. (1963). "Hume On Evil". *The Philosophical Review*, 72(2), 180-197.

O'Connor, D. (1996). "A Reformed Problem of Evil and The Free Will Defense". *International Journal for Philosophy of Religion*, 39(1), 33.

Plantinga, A. (1974). *The Nature of Necessity.* Oxford: Clarendon Press.

Plantinga, A. (2004). "Supralapsarianism, or "O Felix Culpa"". *Christian Faith and the Problem of Evil*, 1-25.

Plantinga, A. (2009). "Transworld Depravity, Transworld Sanctity, & Uncooperative Essences". *Philosophy and Phenomenological Research*, 78(1), 178-191.

Putz, O. (2009). Love Actually: "A Theodicy Response to Suffering In Nature. In Dialogue with Francisco Ayala". *Theology and Science*, 7(4), 345. Retrieved from http://www.informaworld.com.ezproxy1.lib.asu.edu/10.1080/14746700903239502

Reichenbach, B. R. (1988). "Evil and a Reformed View of God". *International Journal for Philosophy of Religion*, 24(1), 67-85.

Rowe, W. L. (1979). "The Problem of Evil and Some Varieties of Atheism". *American Philosophical Quarterly*, 16(4), 335-341.

Stackhouse Jr., J. G. (2001). "Mind Over Skepticism". *Christianity Today*, 45(8), 74.

Trakakis, N. (2008). "Theodicy: The Solution to the Problem of Evil, or Part of The Problem?" *Sophia: International Journal for Philosophy of Religion, Metaphysical Theology and Ethics*, 47(2), 161-191.

Van Inwagen, P. (2006). *The Problem of Evil: The Gifford Lectures Delivered in the University of St. Andrews in 2003*. Oxford: Clarendon Press.

Wykstra, S. J. (1984). "The Humean Obstacle to Evidential Arguments From Suffering: On Avoiding The Evils of "Appearance"". *International Journal for Philosophy of Religion*, 16(2), 73-93.

Secularization and the Earthly Kingdom of God

Kelly Fitzsimmons Burton, Ph.D.

The story of secularization in the West cannot be told apart from the story of the rise of Christianity. Many have noted a relationship between Christianity and Secularization. Some have described the relationship between "religion" and "the secular" as polarization, and others have seen secularization as the logical outworking, or rationalization, of religious assumptions. Jose Casanova observes that: "in the historical process of secularization, the religious and the secular are inextricably bound together and mutually conditioning each other."[1] Again, Casanova asserts that: "Christianity, particularly Protestant Christianity is intrinsically implicated in the development of secular modernity."[2] Owen Chadwick, in the concluding chapters of his Secularization of the European Mind, says "I will seek to define [secularization] in these terms: 'the relation ... in which modern European civilization and society stands to the Christian elements of its past and the continuing Christian elements of its present.'"[3]

The purpose of this paper is to examine the relationship between Protestant Christianity and secularization. More specifically, what is the relationship between Protestant views of "this world" and the process of secularization? What is the relationship between beliefs concerning the providence of God, the millennial kingdom, and the secularization of the West? It should be noted at the outset that there is much variety within "Christendom" and hence may

---

1   Casanova, Jose, "Secularization Revisited: A Reply to Talal Asad" forthcoming in Power of the Secular Modern: Talal Asad and His Interlocutors, ed. David Scott and Charles Hirschkind (Stanford UP), 14.
2   Ibid., 17.
3   Chadwick, Owen. *The Secularization of the European Mind in the 19th Century* (Cambridge: Cambridge University Press; 1975), 264.

be more than one "Christianity" of which to speak. In addition, the process of secularization is dependent on social factors unique to particular cultures; therefore, it may be impossible to speak of a singular process of secularization. Instead, multiple stories of secularization may be told that are specific to particular cultures. For instance, Casanova notices that there are differences in the secularization process in France, England, Germany, and America.[4] Though differences exist within Christianity, as well as within the process of secularization, these differences may be related to how different varieties of Christianity have interacted with the world.

The term "secular," as defined by the Oxford English Dictionary, means "of or pertaining to the world." The secular is often contrasted with the "sacred" or "religious." "Secularization" is a contested concept as it has been associated with the sociological "Secularization Theory" that has ideological assumptions attached to the definition such that the theory itself has become a vehicle for the process of secularization. Casanova attempts to delineate three sub-theses within secularization theory. He says that "what passes for a single theory of secularization is actually made up of three different propositions: secularization as religious decline, secularization as differentiation, and secularization as privatization."[5] Casanova rejects the "religious decline" and "privatization" theses while affirming the "differentiation" thesis. The differentiation thesis has to do with the "functional differentiation and emancipation of the secular spheres – primarily the state, the economy, and science – from the religious sphere...."[6] Casanova's description of the process of secularization is particularly helpful for this paper. He says:

> Secularization as a concept refers to the actual historical process whereby [the medieval] dualist system within "this world" and the sacramental structures of mediation between this world and the other world progressively break down until the entire medieval

---
4 Casanova, Jose. *Public Religions in the Modern World*. (Chicago: University of Chicago Press, 1994). An interesting study would be to relate differing views of providence within Christianity to the development of different Christian cultures of the West.
5 Ibid, 7.
6 Ibid, 19.

system of classification disappears, to be replaced by new systems of spatial structuration of the spheres. Max Weber's expressive image of the breaking of the monastery walls remains perhaps the best graphic expression of this radical spatial restructuration. The wall separating the religious and the secular realms within "this world" breaks down . . . from now on, there will be only one single "this world," the secular one, within which religion will have to find its own place.[7]

The "breaking of the monastery walls" is something that happens from within a Christian framework. In addition, the differentiation of the spheres, or the structuring of societal institutions, occurs in relation to the previously unified Roman Catholicism.

In his chapter on "The Process of Secularization" in *The Sacred Canopy*, Peter Berger argues that Protestant Christianity, as opposed to Roman Catholicism, has played a considerable role in the secularization of the West. He says that:

> If compared with the "fullness" of the Catholic universe, Protestantism appears as a radical truncation, a reduction to "essentials" at the expense of a vast wealth of religious contents. This is especially true of the Calvinist version of Protestantism, but to a considerable degree the same may be said of the Lutheran and even the Anglican Reformation.[8]

He argues that Protestant reduction of the "sacred" elements of Christianity found particularly within Catholicism, elements such as "mystery, miracle, and magic," led to a "'disenchantment of the world.'"[9] He notes further that:

---

7 Ibid, 15.
8 Berger, Peter. *The Sacred Canopy: Elements of a Sociological Theory of Religion*. (New York: Anchor Books, 1967.), 111.
9 Ibid, 111.

> The Protestant believer no longer lives in a world ongoingly penetrated by sacred beings and forces. Reality is polarized between a radically transcendent divinity and a radically "fallen" humanity that, *ipso facto*, is devoid of sacred qualities. Between them lies an altogether "natural" universe, God's creation to be sure, but in itself bereft of numinosity.[10]

Whether one agrees with Berger's assessment or not, what is interesting in Berger's observation is the differences he draws between Catholic and Protestant understandings of "this world." These differences play an essential role in the secularization of the West.

While both Casanova and Berger accentuate the notion that Protestant Christianity has contributed to the process of secularization in a particular way, it should also be noted that there may be notions contained within the Hebraic worldview that have secularizing implications. Before the monastery walls came down, there was a long historical process that led to their being built up. Berger maintains that the "secularizing potency of Protestantism...had its roots in earlier elements of Biblical tradition." And furthermore, "the roots of secularization are to be found in the earliest sources for the religion of ancient Israel."[11]

Some elements uniquely contained within Hebraic views of God, the world, and man are not found in other cultures of the time. These include the creation of the world by a transcendent God, who is distinct from the created order; God not only creates but he also providentially sustains the creation, and human beings are specially created in the image of God. In this system of belief, humans are free, rational, individually responsible before God, yet living in community and responsible for the ordering of society and culture. The first man and woman were commanded to "be fruitful and increase in number; fill the earth and subdue it."[12] This command has been referred to as the "dominion mandate." The created realm is law-like, orderly, knowable by humans and is a revelation of the Creator him-

---

10   Ibid, 112.
11   Ibid, 113.
12   Bible. *New International Version* (Tennessee: Broadman & Homan Publishers; 1986), Genesis 1:28.

self. In addition, humans had a moral law "written on the heart" by which they were to live (later given by God on Mount Sinai). Within this worldview, the first man had a covenant relationship with God with the promise of life for obedience and death upon disobedience. After the fall of the first humans, God provided a plan to redeem fallen humanity within the historical process. There is a promise that the "seed of the woman will crush the head of the serpent." The work of dominion would now have to include humanity's dominion, not only over the creation but also over sin. It may be argued that the "root" of secularization that Berger mentions lie within some of these elements of Hebraic belief.

Early Christianity builds upon these themes and recognizes Jesus "the Christ" as the "seed of the woman" spoken of in Genesis 3. He is the Messiah who was to crush the head of the serpent, provide redemption for fallen humanity, and usher in the kingdom of heaven. The Israelites were forward-looking, waiting for the coming of the Messiah. This forward-looking attitude provided hope and a sense of the future redemption of this world. Early Christians believed that Jesus was the fulfillment of that hope. He commands his disciples to "go and make disciples of all nations…And surely I am with you always, to the very end of the age."[13] With the belief in Christ's death, resurrection, and future coming, how were the early Christians to live in the world? When would be the end of the age?

Some early Christians attempted to obey Jesus' command to go out into the nations and make disciples, yet they were faced with persecution, Gnosticism, and influences from surrounding cultures. These challenges and influences seem to have contributed to the flight from actively engaging "this world," and the rise of the monastery walls. Christians were facing the challenge of living in the world while not being of the world. Gnostic teachings contributed to a view of the world as neutral at best, evil at worst. Flight from the world in these circumstances is understandable.

In response to some of the challenges of the day, Augustine influenced the thinking of early Christianity with his views on original sin, God's grace, and free will and predestination. These notions would be revived later with the Reformation. His *City of God* is of particular importance for the topic of living in the world. In this

---

13   Matthew 28:19.

work, Augustine speaks of the city of God and its conflict with the city of man. With this work, he sets up a dichotomy between two types of people, a dichotomy that remains in the thinking of many today. Either one is a member of the city of God or the city of man. These cities represent the community of belief and the community of unbelief. Perhaps "the city of God" vs. "the city of man" is the origin of the dichotomy between the "religious" vs. "secular" distinction today. Augustine's two cities seem to co-exist side by side throughout history, between the first and second comings of Christ, with no side particularly victorious.

Some saw the city of God as the Roman church. Casanova notes that: "the unique establishment of a *Civitas Dei* in this world, of a Roman church with real and significant worldly power, which pretended to rule the world directly or indirectly, was of crucial importance."[14] Some within the church had an "otherworldly" asceticism and withdrew into the monastery, while others sought to expand the power of the church in the world. Willis B. Glover, in his work *Biblical Origins of Modern Secular Culture*, describes the long, hard work of the monks to "Christianize" pagan Europe. He argues that: "the medieval centuries were not a period in which Europe was uniformly Christian. On the contrary, this was a period when Europe was in the process of becoming Christianized, and the process never reached anything like completion."[15] Some were attempting to obey the Great Commission to make disciples of all nations. The secularization of Europe could not happen prior to the Christianization of Europe. But, what was the status of Europe before the coming of Christianity? Was it secular? Peter Berger would probably argue that all across Europe people maintained views of the world were "sacred" and the world was "enchanted." Europe was not yet secularized.

Berger sees "Catholic Christianity, both Latin and Greek" as "an arresting and retrogressive step in the unfolding of the drama of secularization, although it preserved within it (at least in the Latin West) the secularizing potential."[16] He sees in the Protestant Reformation "a powerful re-emergence of precisely those secularizing

---

14   Casanova, *Public Religions*, 50.
15   Glover, Willis B., *Biblical Origins of Modern Secular Culture* (Macon: Mercer University Press; 1984), 19.
16   Berger, 124.

forces that had been "contained" by Catholicism."[17] The "secularization of Europe" takes a different form depending on the influences of either Catholicism or various forms of Protestantism in each nation. It also seems to take shape regarding these different "Christianities'" view of this world and the world to come.

The coming down of the monastery walls first occurs in the context of Renaissance humanism and the Protestant Reformation. In some ways, the Renaissance returned to a classical, pre-Christian, view of the world. This return to classical culture was filtered through the lenses of Christianity. Ideas of man as radically free, and God's creation as dynamic, developed in opposition to the medieval view of man in hierarchical relationship to the fixed cosmos. Glover notes that: "Man operating freely in the world was a sub-creator under God, and his creations were the world of history and culture. This was not merely a theory for the classroom or study; it was a mode of consciousness, and it released a burst of personal energy which characterized the period."[18] People became involved with "this world" in a new and exciting way. Humanity seemed to be revisiting the Hebraic view of the "dominion mandate" of Genesis. Attention was paid to the creation in scientific investigations and the development of new technology, and to history, the humanities and culture in "this world." Renewed attention to "this world" helped give rise to the development of institutions and the differentiation of the different "spheres." Glover makes a further observation that:

> By the time of the high Renaissance, the distinctive cast of mind that was to characterize the West to our own time was already formed. In the next century it was to launch that scientific movement that is, perhaps, the most obvious distinctive feature of the culture that has come to dominate the world…Europe was headed for the greatest cultural, religious crisis so far in its history, and science was to have a major part in producing it.[19]

---

17   Ibid, 124.
18   Glover, 61.
19   Ibid, 78.

The Christian view of the world as knowable through empirical study, the human as a rational being, and God as transcendent, thus the creation as contingent and dependent rather than static and fixed, contributed significantly to the rise of modern science. Seeds of classical culture also contributed to the growth of science as well. A return to Greek views of atomism and materialism also contributed to science. The rise of science may not have had exclusively Christian influences, although it was a significant factor. Glover describes the move that was made by the new empirical science to pursue its study "without regard to any historical origins in theology of its basic concepts."[20] A particularly Christian view of the world as knowable, humans as knowers of the world and free co-creators, and creation as dynamic, all helped to give rise to the new science. Glover notes, the "capacity of the order of nature ordained by God to be treated in independence of theology ironically led to its being absolutized into a new world order in which the mechanistic methods of science were converted into a mechanistic metaphysics."[21] The new science was becoming secularized in that it was a "differentiated sphere" separate from the church. However, it was also to become "secularist," in that it was to be the carrier and promoter of a view of the world that had "mechanistic metaphysics" that would become divorced from a view of the Creator/creation distinction.

The rise of modern science has much of its roots in western Christianity. Science and religion have not always been "at war" with one another. Not only did the Renaissance contribute to the rise of science, and other western institutions, but the Protestant Reformation had a major influence on how western institutions were formed. Many of the institutions of western society took shape within the Protestant Christian context. The differentiation of the spheres of society, and the coming down of the monastery walls is partly what constitutes secularization, and this differentiation originally took shape within a Protestant context. Thus, Protestantism is intimately tied to the process of secularization. Peter Berger describes Protestantism's contribution to secularization as the abolishing of the "world in which the sacred is mediated to [the Catholic] through a variety of channels…a vast continuity of being between the seen and the unseen."[22] He goes on to say that Protestantism

---

20   Ibid, 93.
21   Ibid, 93.
22   Berger, 112.

"broke the continuity, cut the umbilical cord between heaven and earth, and thereby threw man back upon himself in a historically unprecedented manner."[23] He argues that Protestantism emptied the world of all possible modes of the mediation of God's grace except for the word of God. He claims that as long as this channel of grace remained open between God and man "secularization was effectively arrested." He says: "it needed only the cutting of this one narrow channel of mediation, though, to open the floodgates of secularization."[24] Once the word of God, as the only means of grace is eliminated, then man is left in the world alone, cut off from an utterly transcendent God. But is Berger's account the only one that may be told? Is his account concerning the grace of God and the view of man and the world accurate? Is this what the Protestant Reformers believed about God and the world?

There are a variety of beliefs about the providence of God and man's place in the world within Protestant Christianity. Does each view contribute equally to the process of secularization? Or do some views contribute more to the process than others? The purpose of the next section of this paper is to explore some of this variety of belief within Protestant Christianity concerning humanity's role in the world, the providence of God, and the kingdom of God.

With the coming down of the monastery walls, the focus in Christian thinking changed from "the other world" to the importance of "this world." Reformers, such as Martin Luther and John Calvin believed that the world of nature was a revelation of the glory of God as much as the written word was a revelation. They held that "human beings cannot know the naked God ... They can only find God in his works and his words."[25] Though God's creation is his self-revelation, Luther and Calvin both held that "one must stand in the right relationship to God to understand creation."[26] God's grace was required to change a person's heart from not seeking, understanding, or doing what is right in the eyes of God to seeking God, understanding his creation and word, and doing what is required of man by the law of God. How does one receive this grace of God? This grace, or as Luther has stated it, "justification" is by faith alone and

23   Ibid, 112.
24   Ibid, 112.
25   Schreiner, Susan E. *The Theater of His Glory: Nature & The Natural Order in the Thought of John Calvin* (Grand Rapids: Baker Books; 1991), 117.
26   Ibid, 117.

that very faith itself is a gift from God. Whether one possessed the grace of God depended on the miraculous change in the heart of an individual through the work of God himself. The Reformers, Calvin especially, revived and placed a new emphasis on the Augustinian view of predestination. God, in his providence, has predetermined who will receive grace. All men are responsible before God, yet those who do receive the grace of God have a particular responsibility in this world. Susan Schreiner notes that for Calvin:

> This gradual internal restoration of the soul enables the believer to find again a richer knowledge of God from the contemplation of nature. This Christian theology of nature cannot be separated from Calvin's understanding of a sanctified, restored order within the soul...With the soul's restoration, nature once again serves God's original purpose: to manifest the divine majesty to the human creation in praise of their common Creator.[27]

Contrary to Berger's "disenchantment" theory of Protestantism, Luther and Calvin believed that the world is a primary revelation of God's nature and glory. Also, God's providence within the world – history itself – is a source of revelation. If creation and providential history are primary texts of God's revelation, there arises a high priority in studying the text of creation and understanding the purposes of God in nature and history. Luther and Calvin both thought that man is himself a revelation of the glory of God. Also, they thought that man could not truly know himself apart from God. This notion, in conjunction with the idea of being predestined, or being counted among "the elect," lent itself to internalization and individualistic focus in religious piety.

Luther's theology of justification by faith alone seemed to lend itself to a more pietistic view of the world than Calvin's. The goal of the Christian life for Luther, once one has been justified by faith, appears to be a pietistic life in this world with the hope of attaining the world to come. Max Weber draws out the importance of the de-

---

27 Ibid, 113.

velopment of capitalism through Luther's idea of a "calling" in this world. He says that what was new in Luther's notion of a calling was that "the valuation of the fulfillment of duty in worldly affairs [is] the highest form which the moral activity of the individual could assume."[28] The way one was to live acceptably to God was to excel in one's moral duties and obligations in this world. And yet, Weber notices, "for Luther the concept of the calling remained traditionalistic. His calling is something which man has to accept as a divine ordinance, to which he must adapt himself. This aspect outweighed the other idea which was also present, that work in the calling was a, or rather *the*, task set by God."[29] For Luther, man had a particular calling in this life, and it was his moral obligation to labor in that calling before God, yet there was no particular view within Luther's theology towards changing the world in which the believer lives. On the contrary, "obedience to authority and the acceptance of things as they were, were preached."[30]

The most significant development of Lutheranism for this paper is the doctrine of the two kingdoms. Casanova notices that: "it was Luther who in his pamphlet *The Freedom of a Christian* had created a radical chasm between the realm of freedom and the realm of unfreedom, assigning freedom to the "inner" man, to the "inner" sphere of the person, while the "outer" person was irremediably subject to the system of worldly powers."[31] He also says that: "Lutheranism introduced the principle of a double morality, a secular one for the outer sphere of the "office" and a Christian one for the "inner" sphere of the person, so that the freedom of the "inner religion" was assured."[32] This pietistic inward turn of Lutheranism preserved the private element of religious life but was detrimental to public expressions of religion. This view also offered no critique of the world and was "immune to the scientific critique of religious worldviews."[33] This world became a place for waiting for the world to come. The doctrine of the two kingdoms was a contributing factor to the secularization of the West.[34] This view accommodated the

---

28   Weber, Max. *The Protestant Ethic and the Spirit of Capitalism* (New York: Charles Scribner's Sons; 1958), 80.
29   Ibid, 85.
30   Ibid, 86.
31   Casanova, *Public Religions*, 33.
32   Ibid, 33.
33   Ibid, 33.
34   An interesting study would be to connect Lutheranism and the particu-

public/private split in religious life and the neglect of the development of this world.

Berger notices that the world, "disenchanted" as it was and cut off from mediating influences, could "all the more rapidly be secularized" and that "the logical development of this may be seen in the Lutheran doctrine of the two kingdoms, in which the autonomy of the secular "world" is actually given a *theological* legitimation."[35] The world left to itself without a conscious, active role for corporate Christianity seeking to change the world would develop along a course set by non-Christian secularists. Either the Christians or science severed from the transcendent God, would have to develop the powers latent in the creation. The creation would not lay dormant, especially as humans had an immediate interest in developing technology and medicine to overcome toil and sickness.

Calvin's view of the world differed significantly from Luther's. For Calvin, the creation was "the Theater of God's Glory."[36] Unlike Luther's focus on individual salvation, Calvin's individual was not to focus on his/her own salvation, but rather on the glory of God. Weber says that for the Calvinist:

> The world exists to serve the glorification of God and for that purpose alone. The elected Christian is in the world only to increase the glory of God by fulfilling His commandments to the best of his ability. But God requires social achievement of the Christian because He wills that social life shall be organized according to His commands, in accordance with that purpose. The social activity of the Christian in the world is solely activity in *majorem gloriam Dei*.[37]

Weber spoke of the Calvinist Christian as the worldly ascetic. He/she was to live as a monk in the world. He insightfully notes

---

lar secularization of Germany. Casanova touches upon the possible unique flavor of the secularization of Germany in connection with Lutheran pietism.
35   Berger, 123.
36   Schreiner, Susan.
37   Weber, 108.

that "the drain of asceticism from everyday worldly life had been stopped by a dam, and those passionately spiritual natures which had formerly supplied the highest type of monk were now forced to pursue their ascetic ideals within mundane occupations."[38] The energies, which were previously directed towards preparation for the life to come, were now directed to the knowing and development of this world. The release of these energies and the development of the world for the glory of God contributed greatly to the organization and development of the institutions of western society. Once again, Schreiner says that:

> Calvin believed that [the] creation is to function as the arena of Christian activity and contemplation. For Calvin, the need for salvation does not leave believers analyzing their own condition; justification by faith and predestination release their energies and direct them outward to the world…Christians are to be active in the ordering of society, the upbuilding of the church, the combating of demons, and the study of nature, not because this world can offer salvation or fulfillment but because these activities express the glory of God within the created order.[39]

At points in his theology, Calvin is ambiguous as to whether the fullness of life is a future life in heaven, or whether knowing the glory of God here and now constitutes the essence of the Christian life.[40] This ambiguity continues to contribute to questions about the goal of the Christian life and the redemption of "this world." If God's glory is revealed in the things that are made, and if God's original purposes for creation stand, then what is the value of this world for the Christian? This question remains for the Christian today and how he/she answers will contribute to the process of secularization in one way or another.

38 Ibid, 121.
39 Schreiner, 122.
40 Ibid, 112. Schreiner insightfully reflects: "it is somewhat difficult at times to see why the resurrection of the body and the renewal of creation are necessary if the immortal soul already enjoys, to a large measure, the joy of God's presence [in heaven]."

The Puritans were the primary carriers of the Calvinistic theology. One author, seeming to follow Weber, calls the Puritans "the Worldly Saints."[41] The Puritans attempted to put Calvinist views of creation and providence into practice in the world. James Morone, in his *Hellfire Nation*, traces the Puritan impulse in American history. He notes that: "the Puritans constructed their society around a crusading religious spirit. They identified a mission: saving the world."[42] The mission began with "a City on a Hill." This city was to reflect the glory of God. It was a city that was to be a light and a beacon to the rest of the world. The idea was that the rest of the world needed redemption too, and Puritan society was going to be a model for the world. The novel idea within Puritan thought seems to be that this world is redeemable and that it is the responsibility of the Christian to be actively involved in the redemption, not only of souls but also of society and culture. This is a big task, but the Puritans believed in the power and grace of God to help them accomplish this task. The mission of the Puritans was connected to an eschatological view of life called post-millennialism. According to theologian J. Marcellus Kik, post-millennialism is a view that:

> ...looks for a fulfillment of Old Testament prophecies of a glorious age of the church upon earth through the preaching of the gospel under the power of the Holy Spirit. [Post-millennialism] looks forward to all nations becoming Christian and living in peace one with another...After the triumph of Christianity throughout the earth [post-millennialism] looks for the second coming of the Lord.[43]

Although there may have been post-millennial believers in other parts of the world, it seems to have taken hold in early American Puritan and Presbyterian contexts. This eschatological view was

---

41 Ryken, Leland. *Worldly Saints: The Puritans As They Really Were* (Grand Rapids: Zondervan Publishing House; 1986).
42 Morone, James A., *Hellfire Nation: The Politics of Sin in American History* (New Haven: Yale University Press; 2003), 33.
43 Kik, J. Marcellus. *An Eschatology of Victory* (New Jersey: Presbyterian and Reformed Publishing, co.; 1971), 4.

part of the "dominant Christian establishment" before 1870. Kik notes that: "it can be stated without fear of contradiction that the *postmil* position was the historic position of Princeton Theological Seminary. The Hodges were *postmils*."[44] Many of the Westminster Divines in England, Jonathan Edwards, and many prominent Presbyterian theologians in America held to postmillennial eschatology. Because these leaders were in prominent positions, many as faculty in seminaries and colleges, they had a broad influence on the culture such that post-millennialism took hold in American thought for a time. It was also the predominant view of many preachers of the Great Awakenings in America. Is there a secularizing impetus within the post-millennial vision itself?

James Morone shows that post-millennialism took two paths of development within American life through the course of revivalism. He says: "On the one hand, the revival fostered individualism, egalitarianism, and a faith in historical progress…On the other hand, the revival kindled that hoary…American passion for uplifting the neighbors. Sin was collective, retribution would be shared, redemption must include everyone."[45] There were tensions between the twin ideals of individualism and collectivism within American society and within the ideal of a "City on a hill."

Christianity has never existed as a unified and singular view of the world, and in the American context, there was never one "Christianity," but a great variety of expressions of the teachings of what believers thought was Christ's. With the great diversity within Christianity, it was difficult for believers to maintain a unified eschatological view. In addition to the divisions within Christianity, in his *Secular Revolution* Christian Smith has documented a growing secularist interest in the power structures and institutions of American life after 1870.[46] The dominant Protestant view of the world and its relation to God began to lose its hold within American institutions, if not in the hearts and minds of individuals.

"Secularism" is defined by the *Oxford English Dictionary* as "the doctrine that morality should be solely in regard to the well-being

---

[44] Ibid, 4.
[45] Morone, 130.
[46] Smith, Christian, ed. *The Secular Revolution: Power, Interests, and Conflict In the Secularization of American Public Life* (Berkeley: University of California Press; 2003).

of mankind in the present life, to the exclusion of all considerations drawn from belief in God or in a future state." By 1870, secularism was on the rise in American life. The history of this alternative worldview is well-documented elsewhere, and so will not be discussed here.[47] What is essential for the present discussion of secularization and postmillennial eschatology is that some authors have noted a connection between the two. Jose Casanova notices that Karl Lowith, "who following Nietzsche traced the genealogy of the secular idea of progress through the internal secularization of post-millennial eschatology."[48] Lowith himself argues for an eschatological view more like that of Luther's two kingdoms. He vehemently argues against post-millennialism because of its view of progress and how secularists have interpreted that view. He notes that:

> The starting-point of the modern religions of progress is an eschatological anticipation of a future salvation and consequently a vision of the present state of mankind as one of depravity, no similar hope and despair can be found in any classical writer describing Athens' or Romes' decay. The eschatological interpretation of secular history in terms of judgment and salvation never entered the minds of ancient historians. It is the remote and yet intense result of Christian hope and Jewish expectation.[49]

Lowith's argument seems to be that secular ideas of progress could not have arisen apart from Christian, particularly post-millennial, views of redemption and progress in the world. The notion of progress was absent from classical views of the world. Hence, the idea of progress within Christianity is a secularizing impulse.

Morone believes that the post-millennial vision for America dies after the Civil War. Interestingly, this is also the beginning of Smith's secular revolution. Does the post-millennial vision die, or does it get transformed by secularist dreams of progress, including the dream

47 See Smith.
48 Casanova, "Secularization Revisited," 15.
49 Lowith, Karl. *Meaning in History* (Chicago: University of Chicago Press; 1949), 61.

that humankind will progress beyond the need for religion where science will be the savior of mankind? Morone says that: "the American millennium would live on as powerful metaphor, as a patriotic faith in American destiny, and as a bleak strain of fundamentalism warning about the end of days. But it would not survive – at least not in the cultural mainstream – as the belief in a literal post-millennial American redemption of biblical prophecy."[50] The vision would live on in a new form in American life in the Social Gospel movement and other utopian visions of life in this world separated from the providence of God. Morone notices that "perhaps there was – and is – a secular dynamic within the Social Gospel urge itself. Keep applying religion to worldly problems and it begins to lose its transcendence, its religiosity."[51] Perhaps Peter Berger was correct after all in saying that Protestantism had "cut the umbilical cord between heaven and earth." And all that is left for secular man is to perfect life in this world.[52]

Protestant Christianity, particularly in its Calvinistic form, not only allowed for but also actively promoted the view towards understanding and developing this world, culture, and its social institutions, all for the glory of God. This view of God and the world gave rise to the study of nature as the theater of God's glory and the development of human potential in that pursuit. It may be argued that science, capitalistic economies, educational systems, the nation-state, democratic governments, and other western institutions developed within the Protestant Christian worldview. That worldview, severed from supernatural providence, also gave rise to secularizing and secularist impulses.

With the rise of secularism, as an alternative worldview, and the pluralization of religious belief within American public life, how now is the Christian to live in the world? Jeffrey Stout, in his *Democracy and Tradition*, says that: "the central task of contemporary Christian political theology is to discern how Christ's rulership [of

---

50   Morone, 214.
51   Morone, 354.
52   It is interesting to study the rise of Marxist utopian views in America as Christian post-millennialism wanes. It would also be interesting to study the rise of Marxism in Germany and its relation to Luther's Two Kingdoms view. Marxism seems to fill a void in "this world" left by both by Lutheran abandonment of the kingdom of "the world" and the Puritan postmillennial vision.

pluralistic] communities manifests itself."[53] He asks, does the Christian abandon this world, or work for its redemption? The answer to this question, on behalf of the Christian, would largely depend upon his/her eschatological view. What is the value of this world? What are God's purposes for this world? What is the goal of the Christian life? It is a valid question to ask the secularist as well, how is the secularist to live in the world, knowing that the institutional structures, empirical mindset and knowability of the world are borrowed capital from a Christian worldview? Christianity and secularism, not only the process of secularization, seem to be intimately tied to one another. How do these radically different, yet culturally related views of reality interact with one another in this world? Can they live side by side, at peace with one another? Or is there something inherent within these worldviews – something akin to a post-millennial impulse – that seeks to totalize to the exclusion of the other?

---

[53] Stout, Jeffrey. *Democracy & Tradition* (Princeton: Princeton University Press; 2004), 103-104.

Bibliography

Berger, Peter. *The Sacred Canopy: Elements of a Sociological Theory of Religion*. (New York: Anchor Books, 1967.).

Bible. *New International Version* (Tennessee: Broadman & Homan Publishers; 1986).

Casanova, Jose. *Public Religions in the Modern World*. (Chicago: University of Chicago Press, 1994).

Casanova, Jose, "Secularization Revisited: A Reply to Talal Asad" forthcoming in *Power of the Secular Modern: Talal Asad and His Interlocutors*, ed. David Scott and Charles Hirschkind (Stanford UP).

Chadwick, Owen. *The Secularization of the European Mind in the 19th Century* (Cambridge: Cambridge University Press; 1975).

Glover, Willis B., *Biblical Origins of Modern Secular Culture* (Macon: Mercer University Press; 1984).

Kik, J. Marcellus. *An Eschatology of Victory* (New Jersey: Presbyterian and Reformed Publishing, co.; 1971).

Lowith, Karl. *Meaning in History* (Chicago: University of Chicago Press; 1949).

Morone, James A., *Hellfire Nation: The Politics of Sin in American History* (New Haven: Yale University Press; 2003).

Ryken, Leland. *Worldly Saints: The Puritans As They Really Were* (Grand Rapids: Zondervan Publishing House; 1986).

Schreiner, Susan E. *The Theater of His Glory: Nature & The Natural Order in the Thought of John Calvin* (Grand Rapids: Baker Books; 1991).

Smith, Christian, ed. *The Secular Revolution: Power, Interests, and Conflict In the Secularization of American Public Life* (Berkeley: University of California Press; 2003).

Stout, Jeffrey. *Democracy & Tradition* (Princeton: Princeton University Press; 2004).

Weber, Max. *The Protestant Ethic and the Spirit of Capitalism* (New York: Charles Scribner's Sons; 1958).

Religion and Science: Deconstructing a Modern Paradigm

Rodney W. Tussing (Public Philosophy Press, 2019). Paperback. ISBN 978-1-7328018-0-6. US $19.99.

The state of the public discourse on the status of religion and science is well known for its antagonistic and unfruitful engagement. The scientific and religious communities stand for the most part alienated from each other; the ability to make progress in reconciling these two spheres of knowledge is and has been at an impasse for many decades. Religion and Science: Deconstructing A Modern Paradigm is an attempt at using philosophy to 'unpack, critique, and deconstruct' (p. 2) the divide between the categories of religion and science. Dr. Tussing unpacks the latent assumptions that religion and science presuppose yet often fail to acknowledge when making claims for the legitimacy of either. The unpacking entails an epistemological study of the presuppositions and assumptions that are uncritically held in religion, science, modernity, and postmodernity. Here is where the philosophical undertaking brings the topic to the historical developments which aided in the formulation of the modern paradigm. It is this paradigm that Dr. Tussing calls the reader to critically analyze in its philosophical, scientific, and theological roles. This critical account provides an exposition of major thinkers and ideas since the rise of modernity until the present. With what may otherwise be a daunting task, Dr. Tussing has excelled exceptionally in lucidity and comprehensibility. His care for making the ideas intelligible to the reader by carefully and presuppositionally laying out the content sets this work apart for the benefit of a wide array of readers. There is a care for the reader which is palpable in its approach yielding an imminently intelligible account intended to benefit the public discourse on religion and science.

The work is systematically laid out in six chapters beginning with definitions and ending with a deconstruction of the modern paradigm by testing its ideas for meaning and providing a path for a new epistemic approach, developed by the philosopher Surrendra Gangadean in his work: *'Philosophical Foundation: A Critical Analysis of Basic Beliefs'* (p. 196). Chapter 1 begins by expositing the meaning of religion as commonly understood in culture and academia. It explains the commonly held beliefs regarding the epistemic foundation that each discipline assumes. Science is the privileged position that holds the authoritative role of being associated with proof, facts, progress, and rationality. Religion, on the other hand, is conceived as fideistic, without a rational account or justification, unsophisticated, and ultimately resting on the subjectivity of its subjects to perpetuate its beliefs. This paradigm defines religion and science in opposition to one another. Science is everything that religion is not and vice-versa. The status of science has gained widespread acceptance in public discourse and institutions of higher learning. Science is public and verifiable, while religion is private and without the ability to prove its veracity. In Chapter 2 it is noted that the main assumptions and presuppositions of religion and science have not been sufficiently identified. In other words, 'much of the dialogue has been largely undertaken without adequate assessment of the presuppositions held by each perspective.' (p. 39). Science for example operates under the assumptions provided by the metaphysical position of material monism—which is also known as philosophical naturalism. This worldview assumes that the material world exists, that it is eternal, independent, self-existing, self-maintaining, and ultimately self-explaining. According to philosophical naturalism, all non-empirical claims and non-material explanations (methodological naturalism) are perceived as non-rational or unjustifiable (p. 68). Religion in its many forms falls under the category of non-rational insofar as it postulates the existence of non-material/spiritual beings or aspects of reality.

Chapters 3 and 4 address the rise of modernity and the Enlightenment ideals of the attainability of certainty in philosophical claims. The analysis begins with the foundationalist and evidentialist projects began by Descartes and Locke (pp. 79-86). Their attempt at providing a method whereby justification for knowledge could be given was later challenged and ultimately undermined by Hume and Kant—both questioned the possibility to know either

God or a transcendent realm (p. 89). Questions regarding ontology (nature of being) were restricted to the world of sense experience. After Hume and Kant, knowledge of ultimate reality was set aside for knowledge claims within the realm of experience. Reason was no longer believed to be either ontological—applicable to being and thought—or transcendental, the highest authority which cannot be questioned but makes questioning possible. Reason became subservient to the realm of experience. It could no longer be used to test worldviews and basic beliefs for coherence and meaning. Coinciding with the limiting of reason's epistemic role, a subjectivist turn began to develop in liberal Christianity when it embraced faith as fideism—faith devoid of objective proof. An embrace of subjectivity, intuitive awareness, and reliance on feelings led theism to embrace non-cognitivism, where religious beliefs are not a matter of true or false (pp. 93-94). Liberal Christianity came under increasing scrutiny: 'Beliefs that had not been questioned for centuries were now under the scrutiny of higher criticism and the enlightened intellect of modernity' (p. 96). These new challenges enabled the modern decline of Christian theism and prepared the way for the ascendancy of naturalism. The two main responses were fundamentally lacking: 1) Reid's Common Sense Realism, which affirms that 'first principles were apparent to the entire human race and that everyone should agree to them' (p. 122), and 2) Kuyper's worldview approach where basic principles in theology must be assumed and cannot be proven. Both approaches ended up in fideism—claiming that proof at the most basic level of metaphysical beliefs was not possible. 'Neither of these theistic responses presented a significant challenge, or defeater, for naturalism' (p. 130).

Once the epistemic and historical developments of the Enlightenment and Christian theism are explained, chapter 5 provides a critical analysis of the modern paradigm. The modern paradigm came under philosophical scrutiny by the development of pragmatism and postmodernism. The ideals of modernity and its claims to universal conclusions resting on epistemological foundationalism were rejected. No God's-eye view, no metanarrative is to assert dominance, and foundationalism was replaced by coherentism—all truth and meaning are reduced to language games. We are trapped in the prison house of language. We lost contact with objective reality. Reason can be used constructively within a set framework of meaning, but it cannot be used to questions the coherence of belief systems as such. Worldviews became incommensurable and relative to their own set of beliefs which reason is impotent to judge.

Chapter 6 provides a deconstruction of the modern paradigm by pointing out the unproven metaphysical materialist assumptions held by science under the modern paradigm. Neither religion nor science have proven their first principles. Both have assumed a first principle—whether God or matter—and have begun to operate from those assumptions. Science has not proven nor can it prove that the material world exists, and that the material world is eternal. Questions of first principles belong to the area of philosophy—not science or religion. Philosophy through the critical use of reason is to test basic beliefs for meaning. The burden is shifted from science and religion to philosophy and the use of reason. It is philosophy which needs to overcome the challenges raised by modernity and postmodernity to reason's ability to know reality. The book culminates by giving proof of how reason can be used to prove the ontological argument and the categories to be used in understanding worldviews and systems of thought. This book points the way to the locus of the problem in epistemology—beyond the modern paradigm of religion and science.

Arturo Gastelum

Faulkner University

The Diversity Delusion: How Race and Gender Pandering Corrupt the University and Undermine Our Culture

Heather Mac Donald (New York: St. Martin's Press, 2018). Hardcover. ISBN 9781250200914. US $28.99.

The motto of the United States of America is E pluribus unum, "out of many, one". The Founding Fathers wished to forge a unified nation out of politically, socially, and culturally disparate colonies, and expected that the assortment of Enlightenment and natural law principles woven into the earliest attempts at nationhood would serve as the focal points for a concentration of shared national life. Out of the many peoples and heritages and mores arrayed along the eastern seaboard of the North American continent, it was hoped, would emerge a oneness of purpose giving out onto a wholeness of political belonging. In the national motto, "E pluribus" is the baseline premise, but "unum" is the goal.

In a country forged expressly of mitigated differences, however, what might happen if the unity, longed for by the earliest Americans, were to be disregarded, and the plurality alone left to shift for itself? What would become of a land in which shared purpose had been abandoned as hegemonic, authoritarian, and deleterious to unfettered freedom, and freedom itself, with its endless panoply of choices spread out before it, installed as the only acceptable paradigm? What, in short, might ensue if the national motto were flipped, and the nation were expected to abide by the new doctrine of "E unius, plures"?

Unfortunately, such speculations need no longer be theoretical. The fruits of plurality without teleology are everywhere to be inspected firsthand. In *The Diversity Delusion: How Race and Gender Pandering Corrupt the University and Undermine Our Culture*, Manhattan Institute scholar and puckish bane of university administrators' existence Heather Mac Donald gives us a detailed view of how a culture of anti-unity—commonly trafficked under the shorthand appellation "diversity"—wreaks havoc on an institution, in this case American universities. Mac Donald shows that as "diversity" has been substituted for truth as the prevailing zeitgeist of academia, there has been a concomitant disintegration not only of learning, but also of lifestyle. Those who want to know what a society without a purpose might look like need only venture (if they dare) onto their local quad and see how things are unfolding.

American college campuses today are at the vanguard (in a manner of speaking) of the breakdown of Western culture overall, a breakdown championed under the "diversity" banner by those who seek civilizational dissolution over the patient pursuit of dispassionate knowledge. *The Diversity Delusion* is a meticulously researched rundown of some of the more mind-boggling episodes at the "diverse" bastions of higher learning over the past few years. Split into four parts—"Race," "Gender," "The Bureaucracy," and "The Purpose of the University"—Mac Donald's book gives us an up-close look at just how badly "diversity" has corroded the order and sanity of the American life of the mind.

The first part, "Race," reveals what can only be described as a new metaphysics, whereby the mystical shards of race-memory divide and conquer Americans, splitting us up into ever more fissiparous "groups" (always quickly subdivided into even smaller bundlings) which are claimed to be at odds over the imagined construct of racial identity. Thoroughly besotted with the "diversity delusion," colleges seek to amplify "diversity" by importing more and more members of the endlessly-fracturing race-divisions, which, as might be expected, only further destroys whatever unity of purpose might have remained at a given institution. The fruits of such policies have been on full display at Evergreen State, Mizzou, the University of Wisconsin, Yale, and every university in between. When students are grouped by subcutaneous melatonin content, whether overtly or (probably worse, as Mac Donald hints) surreptitiously, unity becomes virtually impossible to achieve. In 2019, in the latter days of the diversity metaphysics' grip on college life, the centrifugal forces of race-parsing and race-balancing have produced a climate of paranoia—the new metaphysics' crowning achievement—in which "implicit bias" and "unconscious racism" indict nearly everyone with the taint of possible hostility to the other, equally imaginary race-classes.

Part II, "Gender," reveals that the new metaphysics of furious flux and hostility to unity has been even more deleterious psycho-sexually than racially. Race, after all, is just a secondary characteristic, at best, and so any attempt to fray and then bracket people along pigment-lines will only go skin-deep. Race-politics' damage is delimited by race-politics' inherent inconsequentiality. Attacks on the sexual self, however, cut to the heart of the human person, and so it is in the especially pernicious subset of the new metaphysics, "gender," that we see the worst depredations of the diversity delusion in action. As Mac Donald reports, not only is the myth of a campus rape epidemic ruining lives, the idea of sexual "diversity" itself is like an axe to the taproot of the personality. As the two sexes are driven further and further apart by the new dogmas of "diversity," and as individuals are broken into a rainbow of endlessly-varied "genders" (more than one hundred at last count, but surely more by the time this goes to press), the costs of a culture premised solely on differences are becoming impossible to ignore.

Impossible for everyone except the bureaucrats, that is. In Part III, "The Bureaucracy," Mac Donald shows that the diversity delusion is not just smoke and mirrors. It is also big business. A Gremlin-like army of deans and deanlets—who are active mainly at night creepily surveilling co-eds' sex practices, and who seem to multiply when money is poured on them—fans out across campuses and makes sure that the diversity delusion has seeped into every nook and cranny of university life. Like political attaches to companies in the Soviet military, these diversocrats are charged with ensuring absolute conformity to the ideological mission of the ruling regime. Unlike the Soviet political minders, though, the diversocrats have no grand narrative, such as Marxism, to guide them. In the absence of a workable set of ideas, the default organizing principle of the diversity crowd boils down to money. Diversocrats get very big salaries for their work, and the *Aufhebung* of the diversity delusion into US dollars reveals further the bankruptcy of "diversity" as an organizational framework. Parents, if you want to know why your child's university has become an endless episode of *The Twilight Zone*, you need look no farther than the busybody deanlets and factotum ideologues policing the actions, and the thoughts, of their charges.

The Diversity Delusion ends with a note of hope after the catalog of truly farcical, and occasionally heartbreaking, consequences of diversity-madness' hold on American campuses. It also closes with a central truth about the diversity delusion which, if properly grasped, will pave the way to a return to *mens sana* and the rebuilding of our gutted universities. In Part IV, "The Purpose of the University," Mac Donald rightly points out that, while "free speech" may seem an attractive counter-dogma for conquering "diversity," free speech alone will not suffice truly to educate anyone. As Mac Donald writes:

> Th[e] ideal of the Socratic academy [as lauded, for example, by Princeton professor Robert George] is so reasonable that it may seem foolish to quibble with it. Of course, students should engage with ideas that they disagree with rather than silencing anything that challenges their worldview. But there is a universe of knowledge that does not belong in the realm of "opinion." It would be as absurd for an ignorant eighteen-year-old to say: "I have an opinion about early Mediterranean civilizations, but I am willing to listen to others who see things differently," as it would be to say: "I have an opinion about the laws of thermodynamics, but I am willing to listen to the other side." (242)

In other words, the seemingly obvious counter to diversity, free speech, ends up participating in the same polylogism that has ruined American universities in the first place. It is not the case that all utterances are valid. In a pluriform world, it remains an ineluctable truth that there is a hierarchy of ideas, and not just an assortment of them.

Mac Donald's tacit rejection of polylogism in the closing pages of her fine book opens the door for a consideration of why, precisely, "diversity" can never do anything but turn any organized system into pure chaos. The reason can be found in the writings of Aristotle, for example in Book X of the *Metaphysics*, where Aristotle teaches that "the one is the measure of all things," contrary to Protagoras, who claimed that "man is the measure of all things".[1] Again, in the *Posterior Analytics*, Aristotle shows that universals possess being more than do particulars, from which it follows that there is, necessarily, a ranking of things, with metaphysics being at the top of the sciences.[2]

Those who really want to refute the diversity-deluded with a gale of solid thinking will have to turn to the Scholastics for such a knockout blow. For example, as Peter Redpath points out in *The Moral Psychology of St. Thomas Aquinas*:

> St. Thomas maintains that diversity and distinction exist in things so as to represent, as far as possible, divine perfection.[3]

Further,

> According to St. Thomas, just as every existing thing is an imperfect likeness of God, so, too, is every created principle existing in things. [...] In a composite material whole, form exists as a principle generating and uniting a disparate multitude to constitute them as parts of a whole. Considered as such, form constitutes the principle of all qualitative diversity, beauty, and goodness within a material body. By generating the harmony of the parts existing among and within the relation of one part to another part and all the parts to the composite whole, the form causes a kind of perfection, beauty, and goodness within a composite whole through which different parts unequally manifest and replicate divine perfection, beauty, and goodness in terms of the unity, proportion, and clarity with which the form operates in and through them.

---

1 Metaphysics, Bk. X, Ch. 1, 1053a 17-18; 35-36
2 Ibid., Bk. I, Ch. 24, 85b 18-20
3 Peter A. Redpath, The Moral Psychology of St. Thomas Aquinas: An Introduction to Ragamuffin Ethics (St. Louis, MO: En Route Books & Media, 2017), 53, citing St. Thomas, Compendium theologiae, 1, chs. 101-103, and Summa contra gentiles, Bk. 1, chs. 28-29 and 37-41

Considered in this way, the current crop of diversity-delusionists is but the bitter harvest of the Cartesian pseudo-Enlightenment, the rejection of God and the replacing of Him by man. This is to say, the diversity-delusionists make the same mistake for which Aristotle chided Protagoras—they make man the measure of all things. Doing this leads inevitably to chaos.

But why should this be so? It will not do simply to appeal to divine decree as a response to the diversity regime. There must be something more, something of greater detail and intricacy, to stand in opposition to the anti-cosmos of diversity ideology. Luckily, Redpath provides that, too, again appealing to St. Thomas.

> According to St. Thomas, chiefly following the teachings of Aristotle and Pseudo-Dionysius the Areopagite, th[e] inequality of qualitative ability (*virtual quantum ability*) of a form to receive existence accounts for the differentiation in diversity of all genera and species (of all organizational wholes) within the created universe in a twofold way: 1) Imperfect power of form fully to receive and possess existence divides the created order into genera of immaterial and material forms (perfect and imperfect receivers). 2) Imperfect power of matter fully to receive and possess form divides the material order into sub-genera ranging from the perfection of the animal genus, the rational animal (man) to the most weakly existing composite material substances. [...] Forms are diversified as enabling means for receiving a perfection in being: the act of existing. [...] Forms cause diversity in things *by causing a hierarchy*, order, *of perfections and imperfections in receiving the act of existing: a diversity of perfection in having existence.*[4]

---

4   Redpath, The Moral Psychology of St. Thomas Aquinas, op. cit., 54-55, citing Summa theologiae, 1, q. 5, a. 4; Commentary on the Metaphysics of Aristotle, Bk. 12, Lect. 12, nn. 2629-2261; Compendium theologiae, 1, chs. 71-73 and 101-103; Commentary on the de Trinitate of Boethius, q. 4; Summa theologiae, 1, q. 42, a. 1 and 1-2, q. 52, a. 1, reply; Commentary on the Metaphysics of Aristotle, Bk. 5, Lect. 18, nn. 1036-1038, and Fran O'Rourke, Pseudo-Dionysius and the Metaphysics of Aquinas (Notre Dame, Ind.: University of Notre Dame Press, repr. of 1st paperback edn., 2010)

In short, there is order in the world because the world was created by God, and unity is essential to order because there is an inherent sorting of various things based on the extent to which they attain to the genus- and species-perfections available to them. A society which rejects both hierarchy and degrees of perfection—an "absolutely relativistic" society, that is, which declares positivistically that there are no degrees of good and evil—invites in with its cavalier attitude toward truth precisely the bedlam of disorder that now prevails in our formerly respectable institutions of higher learning.

In the pandemonium, though, there is a strange kind of promise. *E unius plures* has, objectively, failed. American universities show with stark clarity that diversity is a toxic ideology and must be rejected as an organizing principle—*cannot be*, in fact, an organizing principle. Reading Mac Donald in tandem with Aristotle, St. Thomas, and Prof. Redpath shows why diversity is the royal road to civilizational ruin, and worse. *E pluribus unum* must remain the motto of the United States and the goal of any sane society. How that longed-for unity is to be achieved can be found by returning to the wisdom of the ancient and medieval philosophers, and Mac Donald is to be commended for diagnosing, one hopes finally, our diversity delusion, and for pointing us out of our current state.

Jason Morgan

Reitaku University in Chiba, Japan.

www.ingramcontent.com/pod-product-compliance
Lightning Source LLC
Chambersburg PA
CBHW050302010526
44108CB00040B/2164